GOD IS SPEAKING

PROPHECY

REVELATIONS

DREAMS

VISIONS

Given to

Robert Turner Claiborne

Copyright © 2014 by Robert T Claiborne
All rights reserved

God Is Speaking
Robert T Claiborne

ISBN: 1495998665
ISBN-13: 987-1495998669

Printed in the United States of America

This book is protected under the copyright laws of the United States of America. This book cannot be copied or reprinted for commercial gain or profit. The use of quotations or copyright for personal or group study is permitted and encouraged. Permission will be granted upon request.

The Scripture quotations are from the King James Version of the Bible. Please note the style capitalizes certain pronouns in Scripture that refer to the Father, Son, and Holy Spirit, and may differ from some Bible publishers' styles.

Take note that satan and related names are not capitalized. We choose not to acknowledge him, even to the point of violating grammatical rules.

GOD IS SPEAKING

Dedication

I would like to dedicate this book to the memory of Ella Fleming, who, in the 1940s-1950s led our family into the work of the Holy Spirit (Pentecostal movement). Also, to my pray mentor, the late Rev. E.L. "Red" Weems, and to the leader of the revival in Wales, Evan Roberts, Mr. and Mrs. Rees Howells and their son Samuel Howells (with whom I had a chance to pray with), and the staff of the Bible College of Wales.

Special Thanks

Helen Joy Dupree, who recorded most of these words, put scripture with the prophecies and put them in print.

Also to Capstone Legacy Foundation in Wayne, PA, Mrs. Nancy Huston Hansen and Mrs. Barbara Howard Miller, who established a prayer room at the foundation where we could stay in prayer daily for the nations and especially Israel.

Endorsements

2 Peter 1:19 "And so we have the prophetic word made more sure, to which you do well to pay attention as to a lamp shining in a dark place, until the day dawns and the morning star arises in your hearts, for no prophecy was ever made by an act of human will, but men moved by the Holy Spirit spoken from God."

We have seen these verses fulfilled in Robert Claiborne's time before the Lord. I have watched Robert seek Him with all of his heart; and I have heard Robert speak those things emanating from the Spirit of God within him which, having heard, we saw confirmed time and time again; either by something written in a magazine, or a blurb on television, or a confirmation in a public place. So we do well to heed these scripture verses, because these are truly words of God, tested in the very confirmations that were seen and revealed soon after they were given. These give support to these verses. As you read these prophetic words, take heed and use them as a lamp lighted in a dark place, in which we are to see the morning star arise. Consider in your heart and believe!

Nancy Huston Hansen
Chairman & CEO Capstone Legacy Foundation

I have known Robert Claiborne to be a man of prayer and fasting during the 20 years of our friendship. Raised in a healthy and lively Christian environment and afterward receiving a first rate education at fine Christian colleges, he then devoted himself to learning the principles of prevailing prayer for revival. He has witnessed the power of prayer for revival since the early 1970's. I have personally witnessed a special movement of the spirit of prophecy in his ministry since January 2013. He stands now as an experienced forerunner in the prophetic-intercessory prayer movement. I encourage anyone called to the prayer movement to read this book and be encouraged. Truly, God is on the move in our day. To Jesus Christ be all glory and honor.

Hayst A. Harrold

Mountains of Salvation Ministries

Burnsville, N.C.

In the years I have known Robert T. Claiborne and witnessed his fulfilling, his calling as a prophet, whether foretelling or forth telling, his words have proven his faithfulness to his calling.

Philip V. Heflin
Apostle of the Faith
Philadelphia, PA.

Robert Claiborne is a gifted prophet, Bible teacher and evangelist. In his new book "God Is Speaking" he describes the times and the seasons of the Lord through prophetic words he has received from God about nations, America, governments, leaders and all segments of society from sports to entertainment. These words provide a true picture of how the Lord is still speaking today to encourage us and prepare us for things to come.

Robert has been a catalyst for breakthrough in my life and for my friends for many years through strategic individual prophetic words he has shared with us privately and at meetings where he is a guest speaker. He has been a very an important prophetic voice for me as I navigated years of challenging times as a lobbyist working with Capitol Hill and related agencies. When wanting to get the most out of life, man turn to personal coaches. Robert is one of the new breed beyond a personal coach that gives you the benefit of prophetic insight and prayer to impact you both personally and professionally. I am glad many will get to know him through the release of this new book "God Is Speaking".

Susan Ironfield

Former Lobbyist

Washington, D.C.

I whole heartily endorse the ministry of Robert "Sparky" Claiborne and this collection of prophecies, dreams and visions. I have known him over twenty-five years in his many tests and trials. He has a sure word from God in this new season. Where ever God has taken him there is always a move of God. He is a prophet to the nations and governments. Read this book and you will find it to be tomorrow's headlines today!

Michael H. Holly

Prophet-Teacher

God Did It Ministries

Capital Heights, MD.

Table of Contents

Foreword   **18**

Section One

PROPHECIES   **19**

CHAPTER 1
PROPHECY YEARS

"The Year of Asia" 2011 And Beyond   23
The Tipping Point   24
Prophecy 2012   25
Prophecy for 2013   27
2015   28
The Year of The Open Door 5774 Israel   31
2014 The Year of The Old Guard Being Deposed   33
2015 The Year of What A Friend We Have In Jesus   37

CHAPTER 2
PROPHECY NATIONS

Cuba   41
"Don't Cry for Me "Argentina"   42
Brazil A Great Nation   43
Korea   44
America's Destiny   46

The Tide Is Turning	47
London, England. UK.	50
Colombia, South America	52
Revival – Europe	55
Word From God – UK – Royal Family	56
London Bridge Is Falling Down	57
Africa	59
The Caribbean	62
Europe	64

CHAPTER 3
PROPHECY CITIES-STATES-SCHOOLS

Move of God	66
My Fire	66
Some Things Which Are To Come!	69
Prophecy for Michigan – Detroit	71
Prophecy for Philadelphia	73
Redeem the Time!	74
The Beauty of His Holiness	75
Top of The Mountain	79
I'm Shaking Philadelphia	84
Glory Cloud Over Philadelphia	86
Intercede for Nations Philadelphia	88
Philadelphia, You Are Mine!	89
Pieces of A Puzzle	90
The Day of The Lord	94
Time of The Harvest	95
The Great Visitation	97

Suddenlies	98
Pillows of Rest	99
The Jews	101
Mercies Everlasting	102
Philadelphia Lawyers/Philadelphia Evangelists	103
More Ready Than You Think!	105
There is A Fire Burning	107

CHAPTER 4
PROPHECY GOVERNMENTS, MEDIA, FINANCES, SPORT, COMMERCE, ETC.

Destiny of A People	110
Fall of False Gods	111
Raising up A People	112
Broken Walls	115
Exposed!	116
Time, Time, Time	118
Pope Removed – Elite Exposed	119
Unraveled – Revealed	123
Prayer Burden	124
"My Little Ones" U.S.A	130
Mysterious Events	132
Checkmate	134
Future Events in Nations	137
Smoke and Mirrors	139
Future Events	142
Israel - Temple Rebuilt	143
War, Earthquakes and Famines	145

Humpty Dumpty	145
Tip of The Iceberg	148
Is Anything Too Hard?	151
War and War	152
The Die Has Been Cast	154
Master Tool and Die Maker	154
Times and Seasons	156
The Boomerang Effect	159
Political Shift	160
Unity	162
Grace	165
Chicken Little - The Sky is Falling	166
The Cry of The Oppressed	168
A House of Cards	169
Age of Gentiles	171
The Greater Works	175
Shock Waves	176
That None Should Perish	178
Prepare for The Unexpected	180
Days of Crisis	181
Rocking Like The Train	183
Jack and Jill	185
Days of Destruction	187
The Hands of the Enemy	190

CHAPTER 5
PROPHECY CHURCH - JEWS

Yokes Broken	192

Words of Comfort	192
Time of The Supernatural	194
My Wealth!	195
Ananias and Sapphira	197
Body Coming Together	198
Wheat and Tares	200
Breaker Anointing	201
Sit At My Feet	202
Honor Me!	203
God's Voice	205
In The Beginning	208
Word of Correction	209
The False Shepherds	212
Homosexual Abomination	213
Let Me Wash You	214
Coming Soon To a Theatre Close To You	216
I Will Make a Way	218
Ministry Leader	219
Stay in My Presence	223
Days of The Supernatural	225
My Father's House	226
Changes	228
I Am Coming Soon	231
The spirit of the anti-christ	232
The Hireling Spirit	234
The Masquerade Party	236
The Greatest Rescue	238

Section Two
REVELATIONS   241

End Time Insights	243
Peace Symbol – Symbol of The antichrist?	245
New Financial Systems	246
Wisdom of The Ages	247
Liar Liar	250
"Issachar Generation"	255
The Old and The New	257
A Flame of Fire	260
End Time Events	263

Section Three
DREAMS   265

In The Classroom Situation With Hitler	267
A Series of Dreams	268
Martial Law Washington D.C.	271
The Stage - Dream – Washington, D.C., 1996	273
Dream Of Trip To Bank in Switzerland 2000	273
A View Of The World	274
Economic Crisis Europe	275
Dreams Of Hometown And War…	276
Washington's Vision	277
Rebirth Of The Holy Roman Empire	278
The Hidden World Rulers	281

Section Four

VISIONS   **283**

Vision Of Moon And Islam	285
Weapons Technology	286
Angel With Gifts	287
Pockets of Devastation	287
Ash Fallout	289

Foreword

It is indeed a signal honor to write a foreword to this incredible book of prophecies.

My friendship with Bob, also known as Sparky, goes back to the early nineties when I was looking for prayer partners. I had arrived from Guyana in the mid-eighties and was attempting to connect with people who loved to seek God. I went to a church social and wandered outside the building to find a tall serious-looking brother who, though he was a member of the church, was outside fasting while his brethren were feasting.

We decided to start a men's prayer group and almost every Saturday night for the next dozen years (except when Bob was out of town), a growing number of believers met mostly in my home to pray for Washington, D.C.

Every Saturday, God would show Sparky visions and revelations about the city, the Congress, the United States Army, the United States, China, Germany and people who attended the prayer meeting. One night Prophet Sparky prophesied that God had called me to be an Apostle and this was corroborated many times by prophets who did not even know me. He was white and I was black but we were glued together by the Holy Spirit for the work of the ministry, even to preaching in the prisons and ministering to the brothers when they were released.

Like the prophets of old, Robert was not promoted by the leadership of his own church but he spoke accurate, edifying prophetic words to grateful and enthusiastic people outside his church for well over a decade before finding acceptance among God's people in Pennsylvania. Though he did not function as a prophet in his church, he would be used in a remarkable way in Brazil and Colombia and in churches that invited him. Finally, he paid a price for his anointing--rejected by the establishment, suffering greatly financially and in his personal life. Then the big break came, and he found a beautiful bride in Colombia, South America. As an apostle who has been used of God to plant several churches in South America, I wholeheartedly endorse Robert "Sparky" Claiborne as a genuine 21st Century Prophet of God.

May the body of Christ heed the warnings and revelations God has given to him about cities and nations of the world!

In the Master's Service,
Apostle Cleveland Harry
President Life Missions International
Washington, DC.

Section One
PROPHECIES

CHAPTER 1
PROPHECY YEARS

"The Year of Asia" 2011 And Beyond

January 22, 2011

The Lord is saying the last chapter in a book of the last 5 years of the earth is finished. Now is opened the pages of a new book concerning the history of the world. We are not even in the first chapter yet, only in the introduction part of the book. The title of the first chapter is evangelization. The Lord says this year shall be known as the "year of Asia" from this year and beyond the focus shall be on Asia. Three important nations to watch shall be Russia, China, and India. There shall always, be a Russia, but the Russia of the future shall be a very different Russia. China in asserting herself and on God's timetable is ahead of its time. God will bring it down a notch and deal with China in a special way. There shall be a border war with Russia and to a lesser degree India will be involved. China will suffer and be defeated and every one will know it is still a paper tiger. In the world, some nations shall no longer be nations and in their place new nations shall rise up and many will have Christian leadership. Some nations that were once enemies of the USA shall now be our friends and some countries that were our friends will now become our enemies. Whole nations shall come to the Lord in just a matter of months. How can this be? I am the Lord God. Nothing is impossible with me. Many coming to the Lord in China, India, and Indonesia other Asia countries and yes Japan to some degree. This is the time for EVANGELIZATION, especially in India now is the time to go. There is an open spiritual heaven and the people will receive, believe and except him as Lord and Savior. This is a whole new time in the history of the earth. A new season! Now is the time to move for me and pray and see the nations in Asia come to me in great power and deliverance.

The Tipping Point

July 08, 2011

In this next book of the history of the earth; which started in 2011, the first chapter's title was "Evangelization." Evangelization shall continue and focus on Asia. Chapter two will be called the "Tipping Point." The most profound, unusual, and earth shaking events will happen this year. Many upset of political systems and nations. Many nations, organizations, corporations, stock markets, etc. shall be weighed in the balances and found wanting (Daniel 5:26).

Many nations God will number and they will be finished. Others shall take over the spoils of these nations, businesses, etc.

We have been in the last days or the end of this age, but in 2012, the last period of the last days shall begin. Weather and national upheaval will affect everything people will do this year. I told you that in 2011 I would turn the apple cart upside down and that everything would be topsy-turvy-helter-skelter religions, government, politics, economies, societies, businesses, and so on would be effected. The apples will be rolling everywhere and impossible to re-gather them. Those you will find and recover will be too bruised to use.

In this hour, our upside down is God's right side up.

Prophecy 2012

November 04, 2011

"The earth is the Lord's and the fullness thereof, but the god of this world would seek to bring chaos into these last days when the fullness of time is even at hand. This year shall be a year of betrayal and intrigue in governments and also the Church and the Nation of Israel. Many secret plots and schemes will be revealed. Many puzzled and complicated situations will be revealed. A power grab! An extremely dangerous time for the USA and our fragile republic. I heard the word, "War! War! War!" (2012 or later?) It's close at hand. Destruction as the world has never seen. This is a season of extremes even in the weather and the whole earth shall seem to quake, shake and roll as never before.

Abide in Me as I abide in you. Let My words abide in your heart and speak them out. Let your abode be with Me and you will find peace, rest and safety as you sojourn in the earth. Be not in fear but walk in the God kind of faith. Yes, My glory shall cover the whole earth as I move by the fire of My Spirit. There shall be a brush fire of My Spirit that will sweep the whole earth. Nothing shall stop the fire of My Holy Spirit as it burns in every corner of the globe. Men who are great in their own narrow eyes shall try to stop it. Governments will try to stop it. Commerce will try, but I will bring it to a halt for days at a time. And yet, the religious shall try, but who is like unto Me? Who shall stand against My face? I Am He who sits above the circle of earth. I laugh as men look like mere grasshoppers to Me. My people shall have a huge voice in many nations and as they set their faces like a flint they will do My greater works: signs, wonders, miracles, the sick healed and the dead even raised shall be common place in the nations.

Don't concern yourself with Russia, China, and the nations of Islam, because already I Am starting to deal with them. The danger to the USA and the world shall be Continental Europe, as France and Germany work against the true believers and the Jewish people. Much evil shall flow out of Germany once again. So rejoice! Because your redemption is even at hand. Fear not, for I AM with you even to the end of this age. Behold, I come quickly and will not tarry. Be ready! Look for Me!

(Russia) Gorbachev is working in the background for one world government.

Prophecy for 2013

October 20, 2012

My children know that 2013 starts the year of the "Great Race." It is a race against time because we have gone into the last of the end time days. We are almost at the end of this age and time is running out. From now on your life will be very different. This country shall be changed and you will hardly recognize it. Yes, there is this great evil in this bountiful land and the world at large. But where sin abounds grace does much more abound. Even as we go into the final months of 2012, this is a time of transition into the new that shall be your destiny that I have prepared for you. I am putting the final details, yes, the last minute touches on you, My "Bride." My Glorious Church who shall be without spot or wrinkle. I am saying "Come to Me, My Beloved." For the days are shortened and all the earth shall see My Glory. And many shall be caught up into the Glory Cloud.

So I charge you to keep your eyes steadfast fixed on the prize. Keep your gaze on me and you will not be deceived or swept away in the dangerous period that the world at large is going into. Remember the high calling you have in Christ Jesus. So run the race as Paul, the Apostle, did with great faith and patience and you will win the prize – the victor's crown.

Faith and Patience will be the power twins for you. Yes, remember when we see Him we shall be like Him. Yes, in a twinkling of the eye we will be changed. Yes, you shall go from glory to glory for all eternity, precious ones. So prepare for the dawning of a new day, a new season. Yes, the end is close and you shall walk in My Power and Glory as overcomers. Behold, I come quickly and will not tarry.

2015

June 17, 2013

Oh yes, yes, yes. Oh, 2013, yes - it shall continue to be a time of transition. It shall be a time when you shall get your house in order. For truly you shall see many awesome things start. And I would even give you this scripture in Isaiah 51:16: "And I have put My words in your mouth; and I have covered you with the shadow of My hand, that I may fix the new heavens as a tabernacle and lay the foundations of a new earth, and say to Zion, you are My people. So you are My people. And I prepare a new heaven and a new earth. I put My Word in your mouth, so speak it out. And you shall truly see what I shall do for you.

Revelations 21:1: "Then I saw a new heaven and a new earth, for the former sky and the former earth had passed away. And there was no longer any sea."

Isaiah 66:22-24: "As for the new heavens and the new earth which I make remain before Me, says the Lord. So shall your offspring and your name remain, and shall be that from one new moon to another new moon and from one Sabbath to another Sabbath. All flesh shall come to worship before Me, says the Lord. And they shall go forth and gaze upon the dead bodies of the rebellious men who have stepped against Me, for their worm shall not die, their fire shall not be quenched and they shall be an abhorrence to all mankind. So truly know that this is the time and a season when you need to arouse yourself, when you need to wake up, when you need to sound the alarm; for it is a different time, so get your house in order in 2013. For 2014 oh yes! The big war and the little war is surely coming, but the timing of this war depends on those actors who would carry it out. So the time is not set as the die is set, but the time shall be soon for things are building up. Things shall develop quicker and quicker. As you go into 2014 and 2015, events shall happen in those 2 years that would normally be events that would happen in 200 or 300 years. But it shall be compressed into 1 or 2 years, for it shall be a time as the earth has never seen developments like this before. There shall be many new developments in technology and war and destruction. But there shall be also the great shaking, but then in the midst of the shaking shall come the great move of God that you've heard about, that we've talked about, that we've prayed about. For the move of God is even at hand. All things that I have promised you are even at hand. But know this: Don't dread or be in fear. All these things must happen that are coming on the earth.

There shall be a shaking; and oh the very elements shall shake. The tornadoes, the earthquakes, the fires, - this is just the beginning. But yet in the middle of this, though you don't know how it could be, but in the middle of destruction shall be the greatest move of God. For I have a people that I have prepared. And yes, I'm bringing in many people, many of My saints into Philadelphia to prepare for that which is to come here. For there shall be a great on-rush of people into this place. For as you know it's a City of Refuge. I have set up other Cities of Refuge around the world where there will be protection for My people and provision for My people. And My people will know to move and go to those places where they can dwell safely. For there shall be an angel over this city. Oh, yes, the angel I told you about that shall blow the great trumpet. Yes, he shall be over this city; along with other angels to protect it from harm. For, yes, in the days ahead you will truly walk every day in a supernatural way. You shall truly be great in the earth and do great signs and wonders for Me. And the evil people, the evil ones, they shall be afraid of you! They shall walk in dread when they see you coming. Those that would not change, those that would not call to Me, they shall flee before your faces, says the Lord Thy God. And even governments shall be afraid of you. Even militaries. Even the great men of this world who give the orders – they shall be afraid of you. They shall walk in dread and in fear; for I shall raise up a mighty army that shall sweep across the whole world. Nothing shall stop what I shall do. But oh, it shall be many days of tremendous happenings: things you cannot even imagine shall happen in 2014. And even as you go into 2015, it shall be the most dangerous time in the world. And soon you shall see My coming; for I shall do a quick work. Don't worry. Don't be in fear for all these things must come to pass. Prophecy will be fulfilled. Many things that you cannot even imagine in 2015 will develop. It shall be earth shaking. It shall shake many to the core. There shall be many suicides of many important people, as they realize what's going on. But know this! Know this! My hand is not shortened that it cannot save or deliver; for I shall be there for you, My remnant people. I shall protect you to the very end. For behold I come quickly and will not tarry, but we shall go through this thing together. I shall be by your side to guide you, but we must go through the greatest time in the earth: the greatest harvest of mankind! For from the north, south, east, west they shall come unto you for help. And know this, and say this, that your help comes only from the Lord!

The Year of The Open Door 5774 Israel

September 05, 2013

Even as this is the Year of the Open Door with the New Year for Israel, 2014 shall be the open door for the church. For the Lord says, yes, yes, there's an open door wide for Israel. There's an open door for My Holy Spirit to come in to Israel this year. Yes, it's an open door to restore to them what's been lost. Oh yes, they shall start to receive. For you shall see in the future that most of the world's billionaires will come from Israel. I will raise up many wealthy people even in the Body of Christ to finance the Gospel. For there shall be many parallels from this day forward, from this New Year on to when you go into the Gentile New Year. There shall be more and more parallels between the Body of Christ and Israel. For the Lord says they shall walk closer together in the days ahead. For they shall find themselves drawn to each other. And the Jewish people will find the true Christians really irresistible for them in the days ahead. And I will tear down dividing walls between the Christians and the Jews. And I will bring such a move of God in Israel. I will bring such a oneness, such a unity. And the Lord says Israel shall be restored for what they have lost for many centuries, and for many thousands of years. They shall be fully restored says the Lord thy God. For in the days ahead they shall receive what their inheritance is in the natural, in the physical, in the land, in the prosperity that I have for them. For many inventions, many discoveries, many new technologies shall come out of Israel and also out of the Christian community. For the Lord says earth shaking ideas shall come and they shall flow out of these communities. And you will find in the days ahead, oh yes, you shall see a mighty work flourish out of Israel. And yes, the Lord says I AM preparing the nation of Israel for what is theirs. And nothing shall be able to stop it. For the Lord says, I AM their recompense. I AM their reward. And the Lord says, yes, I love Israel; the Apple of My Eye, with an unfailing love. And in the days ahead you will see truly how I will move and bless them and protect them. For that which is coming is dangerous, says the Lord. And I shall protect them. I shall protect them. And I shall raise up the Body of Christ to protect them in many nations in the days ahead. For it shall be difficult and it shall be dangerous in many places for the Jews. And I shall raise up the Gentile believers, the true believers, the remnant people to protect them and to deliver them unto Israel, says the Lord thy God. So the Lord says, fret not, worry not, for the great things that shall come upon the earth. For I AM in them. For I shall use many events in the earth for Israel's good. And what the enemy has meant for evil, I shall truly make good out of it. For the enemy is trying to destroy the Body of Christ. The enemy is trying to destroy the Jewish people. But the Lord says I shall restore both communities and bring them together even as one, says the Spirit of Grace.

*Romans 11

2014 The Year of The Old Guard Being Deposed

December 13, 2013

2014 shall be a very important year, for the Old Guard shall start to be exposed and deposed. The Old Guard in governments around the world, those that have ruled for generations, they shall be exposed and removed from power. Even in these United States, the Old Guard in the Republican Party and in the Democratic Party, all the ones embedded in the government in Washington, D.C and in other nations around the world, they shall start to be deposed. They shall be totally exposed and done away with. Governments for days shall be turned upside down. And you shall see that even the election this November shall be very significant, because the Lord says, out with the old and in with the new.

Yes, the Lord says, I have many people that I have hidden for such a time as this that I shall bring in to this government and in other governments around the world at this time. It shall truly be a time of upset in the financial markets, even as they see what's going on in the governments. For all the governments around the world shall be totally in one way or another seem to be totally undone and in confusion, and doing off-the-wall things. For the Lord says yes, I shall bring in the New Guard and they shall be My Guard.

For the Lord says this is a different time and a different season in the earth. And in the Church, the Old Guard shall I start remove in this New Year of 2014. The Old Guard in the Church, those that are corrupt, those that are teaching religion, those that are in adultery, those that are in it for the money, the Lord says I shall remove their candle. It shall be done away with. I shall totally expose many ministries this year. I shall totally expose what they're doing and there shall be such an upset in the religious community. The Lord says I shall bring in My Remnant People in places of authority in the Church starting in this New Year of 2014.

The Lord says I AM coming. I AM coming first to clean out the Church. Then the Lord say, I shall clean out the Government. Then the Lord says I shall clean out the Schools. Then I shall clean out the Militaries, all around the world I AM starting to move in this year 2014. Yes, you shall start to see those in many governments that are Communists. You shall start to see them exposed and done away with.

I AM going to totally undo the Government in these United States. The Emperor, you've heard, has no clothes. There shall be many in the Senate. There shall be many in the House of Representatives. There shall be many in the Judicial Branch and the Executive Branch all throughout this government and in other governments of the world where they shall be totally exposed and they won't have any clothes on.

The Lord says I AM going to de clothe them. I AM going to take their clothes off and the Lord says I AM going to show who they really are. And the Lord says when you take their clothes off, you will see that they're red – you will see that they're Communist. But the Lord says I AM going to totally have My way in the governments, in the schools and universities. Those that have tried to subvert this great land that I have raised up, I shall expose them and do away with them. For they shall not stop the move of God. For I want to one more time send the young people around the world to be missionaries. And I shall have such a move of God in the major universities. I shall cast down the intellectual spirit. I shall cast down the Marxist spirit. The Lenin spirit. And I shall remove those professors that are teaching that or else they shall be born again. They'll be delivered and set free.

The Lord says I shall use the universities once again to send the brightest people out to preach My Good News. I shall raise them up. I shall do a quick work, says the Lord thy God. So the Lord says, this shall be a year of turmoil. This shall be a year of confusion. But in the midst of confusion, in the midst of turmoil, in the midst of one disaster after another disaster this year, I shall move and I shall have My way. Get ready for the War that's coming suddenly. Get ready for the War. Get ready for the move of God that's coming suddenly.

The Lord says yes, and as you go into 2015, it shall be the most dangerous year the world has ever seen. But the Lord says know all of this that what's happening in 2014 and 2015, I AM really with My people; My Remnant People. For I shall raise them up. And the Lord says forget not Israel, to remember Israel. Cover them in prayer. For the Lord says this is the most dangerous time for the Jews in the existence of their history. The Lord says I AM really with Israel and I will be with the countries that support Israel in this time. So the Lord says be not in dread or fear; for behold all these things must come to pass and I AM coming soon in all My power and glory.

2015 The Year of What A Friend We Have In Jesus

December 12, 2014

2015 is a year of what a friend we have in Jesus. The Lord is saying, remember that old song, "What a friend we have in Jesus? All our sins and grief's to bear." Yes, what a Friend we have in Jesus. Yes, the Remnant people and Israel shall realize what a Friend they have in Jesus! For the ride this year for the world will be like riding a wild western bronco. For it shall be quite a ride with the ups and downs. Sometimes the rider on the horse falls off the horse. And so it shall be that with this year, maybe you're thrown off the horse, but you'll get back up and ride it again, and tame that horse. For the Lord says, I shall tame this year of 2015 like a cowboy would tame the bucking bronco. For the Lord says yes, Ride! Ride! Ride! For it's a wild ride this year. It's a dangerous year says the Lord thy God unto you. The most dangerous year you have ever known of. And such a dangerous year for the body of Christ. Such a dangerous year for Israel. But Israel shall realize that they are alone. But they are not alone. For they shall realize that though the nations around the world are opposing them; and even the United States government is opposing them, they know that they have many true friends in the United States. For they will come to realize more and more every day that the true believer is really for them, and is praying for them, and is ready to walk hand in hand with them.

So you shall see many, many Jewish people around the world; but particularly in Israel shall come to know the Messiah, Jesus Christ, this year. They shall accept Him as their personal Savior. More and more their eyes shall be opened, particularly in the nation of Israel, and to a lesser degree many other Jewish people in the world. But many Jewish people shall start to feel the urge and the necessity to move to Israel and the more Israel is squeezed this year, the Lord would say, the more they shall shine. For they are developing new technologies in every field, for even in their military technologies now there are many new things they won't even share with the United States because they feel threatened. And the Lord is giving them secret plans and telling them not to share with anybody; for they shall have secret knowledge that God, Himself, is imparting unto them for economies and for militaries. For they shall be a self- sufficient nation. The Lord says a little is a lot with God, and even as I took the little things, the insignificant things, when the Jewish people were in the desert, when the Jewish people were fighting in Canaan's land a long time ago, I took the small. I took Gideon's army and defeated a mighty host. And I shall take a small nation and I shall defeat many evil hosts that would come against them – the goat nations that would come against them. I will separate them out and I will destroy them and Israel will have the spoils. For the Lord says even though it's a dangerous year, the Body of Christ will prevail! For they'll get back up on the bucking horse again! Israel shall get back up on the bucking horse again! And the Lord says it shall be in the end a great year for the Body of Christ. It shall be a great year for Israel. I AM close by your side. I will never leave or forsake you.

And the Lord says, yes, be bold for Me this year. Be courageous for Me this year. In the face of persecution from other Christians, in the face of persecution from governments, the Lord says, abide in Me. Rest in Me, I'm your sure provision. I'll never leave or fail you. I'll never forsake you. I'll be with you to the very end. For the Lord says this is your year to shine. This is your year to come forth. This is the year of many suddenlies. And you shall be shocked at what shall take place this year. And Great War is coming such as you have never seen. The Lord says, My Remnant people, I will protect. This is the time and this is the new season for sudden change is coming to Israel. Sudden change is coming to the Body of Christ. And the Lord says this is your year to shine. This is your year to come out of the shadows. This is your year to flourish. Yes, My Remnant people, I AM with you this year. I shall be with My chosen people, but I shall be with the Body of Christ. And I shall bring through many circumstances and situations and much evil in the earth, I shall bring My Body and the true believers in Israel, together. Look for the eyes of understanding to be opened as they start to see the Messiah more and more every day.

So rejoice. This is the start of the great move of God. Even this year you shall see many signs that point to the great move of God. For soon there shall be an unveiling of My power and

My glory. And you shall start to walk this year in great power and authority in the earth. Yes, My believers shall start to walk boldly in the earth. And the governments and the nations and the evil ones shall be afraid of My people as they walk boldly in the earth this year. So the Lord says rest in Me. Abide in Me. For My Little Ones shall not be put to shame, but they shall rise up this year. This is the year of great change. It shall be a wild ride. It shall be My year when I shall move. And you shall tame the bucking bronco says the Lord thy God. You shall tame that horse and even ride it. It shall be a beautiful horse after it is broken. And the Lord says, your spirit will not be broken, but the horse's spirt will be broken. For this is the year of the bucking bronco, but the Lord says Jesus shall surely have His way on earth in this hour.

What a Friend we have in Jesus. All our sins and grief's to bear. What a privilege to carry everything to God in prayer. The Lord says yes, relax. Relax. Be not stressed out at all the happenings this year. For in many areas it shall be a difficult year. But the Lord says relax. This is your year. This is your season. And I shall protect My remnant people and Israel this year. A great year it shall surely be, says the Lord your God.

CHAPTER 2
PROPHECY NATIONS

Cuba

November 10, 2012

"Onward Christian Soldiers"

So you think the "C" in Cuba stands for Castro Brothers or for the communists? No, it stands for Christ! Jesus Christ shed His blood for Cuba. So, "Onward Christian Soldiers, marching as to war, with the cross of Jesus going on before." Forward into battle see His banner unfurled. All Christ's foes in Cuba shall be defeated and banished! Onward Christian Soldiers! Keep marching; for the battle will soon be won. Don't get caught up in the physical battle, which will soon take place, but stand in the spiritual battle in prayer, fasting and watching. The weapons of your warfare are not carnal, but mighty to the pulling down of every stronghold and everything that would exult itself above God. (2 Corinthians 10:4). Put on the whole armor of God. (Ephesians 6: 10-18) And do war! For a season, things will seem to get worse! This time has already just started. Be encouraged, and look beyond the lack, circumstances, persecution, and suffering. Look to Me, Who for the joy that was set before Him and endured the cross. (Hebrews 12:2) Soon there shall be a spiritual revolution as the demonic rulers in high places are destroyed. Then shall come a move of My Holy Spirit to rebuild spiritual lives and break the spirit of witchcraft! Later, an economic miracle will quickly rebuild Cuba! So be encouraged, My precious saints and prepare the way of the Lord with much praise for the King of Glory is coming! It is a new time in the earth and all old orders of man are being destroyed. No man or government shall be able to stop what the Holy Spirit is doing for we are in the end time day.

STRATEGY FOR CUBA – Go all over the country to the monuments and to the important places where the revolution started, the high places of satan worship, and pray, praise and declare the soon victory. Sing this song "Onward Christian Soldiers" as you go to these places in small groups. Praise Him that it is done and see it with the eye of faith.

Words to song Onward Christian Soldiers.

"Don't Cry for Me "Argentina"
That Old Song

December 14, 2012
Received Early Morning Prophecy

Yes, you should weep for Argentina. For the woes which have started to come on her. I gave you status in the world. Buenos Aires was the Paris of South America, a delightful place. You had a high standard of living and I brought many talented people who longed for a new and better life to your shores. Why did you do great harm to the Apple of My Eye and hide evil ones who tried to destroy all My Beloved Jewish people? You were looked to as a leader by the other countries of South America, but you didn't look to Jesus Christ, but to Peron as your savior! Then you were the first to bring about homosexual marriage to South America. Why can't you understand this is an abomination to Me? What did you drink to compromise your sound judgment? Your leader must go because of her evil deeds. She will just fade away lost in time.

Argentina, your time is up! No longer will you be known as a great nation. Yes, there is a great company of "believers" in your midst who are praying. Yes there shall be one more great move of the Holy Spirit that will shake every class of your society. Then that will be it! Weep cry for Argentina for My heart is broken for you, but your time has run out. Time is running out for all the nations! Rejoice for that great move of My Holy Spirit which is yet to come to the nations of South America. "Behold, I come quickly and will not tarry!"

Brazil A Great Nation

December 14, 2012

Early Morning

Brazil is a great nation in the natural and in the spirit realm. I have a great people who worship and pray unto the God of Israel. I have heard your cry and I AM moving. I AM going to break the yoke of bondage off your nations. Your cry has gone to the highest part of heaven. I AM breaking that Anti-Christ spirit off your great land. The spirit of witchcraft and divination is going! I AM breaking the back of "Carnival!" Your corrupt communist government will soon be gone. I AM going to so break that spirit of communism in South America so that it will be an example to other nations. I have a great company in Latin America who are fasting and praying for this to end. I say, Cuba! Brazil! Venezuela! Bolivia! And Ecuador! Be set free now! Your governments are perverse!

Now I will start with that ridiculous woman in Brazil with a "Jezebel" spirit. I will make an example of her and her mentor, "Lulu." They will be exposed and put to shame! Totally undone! As you have plotted with the enemies of Israel now I will plot against you and bring you to nothing! You have been willful and obstinate in your evil and now is the time of your demise. There shall be a great time of shaking in Brazil and I will bring My true body of believers to the forefront. Soon there shall be a great explosion of My supernatural power and the signs, wonders and miracles shall amaze you! This is My time and no man, woman or government shall be able to stop what I AM doing. Be faithful unto Me, My little ones, for I AM with you even to the end of the age!

Korea

March 25, 2013

The area where North Korea is now located was once a

stronghold for Me in days past. I had a powerful people there who would war in the spirit for all of Asia. Satan really did try to stop all this, but where sin and evil abounds, grace does much more abound. (Romans 5:20) I remember the prayers of the saints who are now with Me in heaven. Is anything too hard for Me? Is My hand shortened that I cannot save and deliver? Even now I have heard the prayers of My weak, precious ones in fear in camps, and prisons, in the North, who lift up their voices to Me in faith, not looking at situations, but knowing I AM well able. I have a mighty company in the South of that nation, for I see the nation as one, who have faithfully for 60 years lifted up one voice to Me to deliver and set the captive free. I have heard their cry and now I will no longer delay My actions. I will move and destroy that evil, wicked government. I would let them stay in their folly if not for My remnant people, who are special unto Me. Even if it takes half the world on the brink of destruction and war, I will do it. I will totally destroy My enemy in Korea and put fear into governments of China, Vietnam, and Russia. There shall be a great spiritual shaking (earthquakes) in Asia and then I will move in a great Holy Spirit move of God that no man or spiritual evil can stop. I shall prosper My Korean people with great wealth so they can fulfill My call to be evangelists to Asia and the uttermost regions of the world! Then, I will come soon!

America's Destiny

May 13, 2013

I have called this nation to have a destiny. To have a destiny – and the destiny is a special nation called unto Me. For I have called this nation to protect the weak around the world. To protect the oppressed around the world. But more than that, I called this nation even for such a time as this, to be a protector of Israel. But I have called this nation to spread the gospel around the world. But they shall reap like a whirlwind......those who have tried to change the course of this nation, they shall reap and be caught up as it were in a whirlwind. For I shall blow with the wind of My Holy Spirit and move them out of the way, tear down their kingdoms, blow away their structures like a tornado would, for I shall have My way in this country. Once again this country shall go to the nations. Once again this country will receive those to come here and be educated in the things of the Spirit and then go back to their nations. For once again I will use this nation. And even in this last days I will stop and reverse the course that has been set for this nation that would go against Israel, but I shall reverse that, and I say they will support Israel. I say they shall once again go to the nations out of this nation; for I shall stop that evil which has come into this nation for decades and decades. I shall put a stop to it. I shall expose it and I shall remove it says the Spirit of the Lord. And I say to you, My remnant people, as you continue to stand in the gap, as you continue to watch on the wall, you shall truly see Humpty Dumpty fall! Oh, yes, you'll see the kingdoms of this earth as they unravel, because I will have My way in the earth in this time. For My Kingdom is soon to come and I AM soon to come in all My power and Glory. And I will have a people here, in this place, I will have a people in this nation that will be waiting for the manifestation of MY glory. For I shall use My sons and daughters, the hidden ones, the little known ones in this country. I shall raise them up as a mighty remnant army and they shall be a mighty spearhead to once again take this gospel to the nations. For the kingdoms of this earth that are arrayed against My people, all the spiritual and earthly kingdoms, they shall truly fall and fail in this time; for I will confound the wise of this world with the foolishness of preaching, says the Lord thy God. I shall preach My Word through you and others like you and great shall My move of God be, says the Lord unto thee.

Linked to prophecy Humpty Dumpty.

The Tide Is Turning

May 20, 2013

The tide is turning. In these United States, the tide is turning. It shall be a rip tide in this country and in the countries of Europe. In England, in particular, there will be a rip tide. A rip tide is one that is a violent tide. Oh yes, yes, yes, it shall be such a time of violence in the spiritual realm and some places in the natural, where this shall take place. In the beginning it shall take place here; even in this country it is taking place here, in these United States, it has begun. The tide of change is here and there shall be a great shaking. The currents shall roll in. The spiritual currents are going to change in this country in such a way that you will be flabbergasted how I do it. I'm going to bring the change in governments and in economic situations. I'm going to bring it in the universities and in the military. I'm going to bring such a change and such a shaking in this country. Oh yes, it shall be a rip tide in Europe. There is going to be such a tide of change in Europe. For a while in Europe, it shall turn and those countries shall move towards Me in a great revival. There shall be an upheaval, but then they will turn back the other way. And then the spirit of Anti-Christ will come in to that place. But the Lord says there will be a great rip tide in the UK and all of those countries. It shall start here. It shall go to Europe. Then it shall go to Asia, to China, to India, to many other countries. The tide will change. Oh, there shall be a time and a season where in many countries there will be a rip tide of violence; when one current meets another current and they butt heads together. But the Lord says, yes, even in Asia there shall be such a time of change. The demonic there shall be destroyed. The false religions shall be destroyed. Yes, it is going to affect everything people do in the days ahead. It shall effect the factories. It shall effect the shipping. It shall affect the making of products in many countries. Oh it shall really effect everything in a way you cannot imagine. But this tide – the tide of the Holy Spirit – it shall flow. The ocean shall flow. The oceans of My grace shall flow. The oceans of My power shall flow. The oceans of My healing flow shall be there for many nations. This is the time when change is surely coming in the earth. It's a change you can't even imagine. Some shall be good changes and some shall be bad. But there shall be great upheavals. There shall be great violence as the two opposing forces, the two different tides, flow in against each other. The rip tide effect, it shall surely be in many countries. There shall be a rip tide here and there shall be a rip tide in Europe and in England.

I shall move in the Commonwealth countries once again; and use them to carry the gospel. Oh, yes, change is surely coming, so be ready for it. Expect it, because suddenly there's going to be many suddenlies. Many suddenlies. Things will seem to change almost overnight. You can't wait to get up the next day and see what I have done in the earth. There shall be such a great awakening in this Philadelphia area. The tides of change are coming to Philadelphia. The tides of change are coming to the government. To every institution. And yes, I shall move in the colleges and universities. There shall be such a tide of change that from the top on down – all the officials, all the professors, shall be shaken, and I shall use these places – these higher places of learning. I shall use them once again. They shall be where the missionaries shall flow out to the nations. For the tide of change is surely coming. So expect My hand to move suddenly. You shall see many suddenlies in the days ahead and you will know it's of Me. So just ride with Me. Go with Me. Pray it in. Pray it in. Believe with Me. Put your faith with Me. And as you pray and as you intercede, so shall the tide and the effects be throughout the whole world. For I AM counting on you, My remnant people, to pray in this move of God. Even as Rees Howells prayed in the changes in World War II, Pray! Pray! Pray! Seek My face. Agonize before Me for the lost and the dying. Oh yes you shall see the tide of change come because of your prayers, says the Spirit of Grace.

London, England. UK.

June 21, 2013

Great Britain, that mighty Empire.

Oh, that the sun never set on. I shall totally bring that government down. The government of David Cameron, I shall bring it down; I shall bring it to nothing. You put the abomination of homosexuality marriage in My face. I shall totally undo you and your government – that British foreign service that has, time after time, turned its back on Israel and the Jews – I shall bring you to nothing says the Spirit of the Lord! Oh, yes, even at this time I AM moving in London. Even where London has been destroyed by fire before, this time the fire of My Holy Spirit shall move in all of London. And it shall even reach and touch the Royal Family and they'll be totally undone. It will reach the Muslims there. The Muslims will be under such great conviction of the Holy Spirit that they will either turn to Me or they'll flee that country, says the Spirit of the Lord. For I shall have My way. I AM starting in London even this day. Even in this season, I AM starting in London. For oh, London, I shall totally take you by force, says the Spirit of the Lord unto you! I shall take you in a violent way. And I shall first of all start to move in the UK and London, and then I will move in the countryside. I will move in the Outer Hebrides Islands, the Shetland Islands, the Islands of Lewis and Harris. I shall move among the weavers, and among the knitters. Then I shall move in Leeds among the clothing people. I shall move among the shoemakers. I shall move on Savile Row. I shall move among the ordinary folks. And then I shall move in the university campuses. Oxford and Cambridge, you are Mine! And I shall turn you into My schools once again, says the Spirit of the Lord, for they are Mine! Once again, you shall take the gospel around the world. So I shall move in the UK. I shall move in Ireland and Northern Ireland. I shall move in Scotland and Wales. I shall stir up the spirit of Rees Howells once again in Wales, and Smith Wigglesworth in England Yes, truly I shall destroy the spirit of alcoholism in that land. Truly I shall destroy that arrogant spirit – that spirit that thumbs its nose at Me......that smug, arrogant spirit. I shall truly bring down that agnostic, secular humanism, that spirit of the Anti-Christ that has come into that country. Yes, I shall totally undo those in the government that have come against My people, and even against My people, Israel. I shall bring you to nothing. Yes, I shall have you and you shall carry the gospel once again to the other nations. You Canada, United States, New Zealand and Australia. In all your wickedness in Australia, in all your wickedness in New Zealand, - you have the same attitude as the motherland. But I shall truly deal with you in a mighty way in the days ahead. These countries shall once again take the gospel around the world, for the revival fires shall move once again in all these countries. Yes, this is a different time and this is a different season. I shall separate you from the other nations of the world and use you. I shall drive out the anti-Semitic spirit from in your midst. Truly you shall be totally undone when I AM finished with you, says the Spirit of Grace. I will have My way once again in your lands. I will make you mighty again if you will only heed My warning and listen to My Voice, says the Spirit of the Lord.

Colombia, South America

June 28, 2013

My faithful ones in Colombia, who rise early to pray and seek My face, what does the C in Colombia stand for? For the world at large it stands for coffee, cocaine, crime, corruption and still for others, communists. But for Me it stands for Christ, compassion, care, companionship and a great company of believers who know, despite circumstances and situations, that Jesus Christ is Lord over Colombia! Christ the hidden One will now show Himself strong for that nation! You are soon going to be the voice of South America, even the voice of Christ for that region of the world and beyond. Everywhere you go in the world you find people from Colombia because you love adventure and you are risk takers. Soon you will be found in almost every nation as evangelists for that is your call and also as ones who bring peace to many situations. You will be My peacemakers! I AM going to increase you in finances and business for soon the way business is conducted will change. You will be in the forefront with new business concepts, for I will give you MY precepts and plans to conduct fair and honest business. Many witty inventions shall come out of Colombia and new deposits of minerals, veins of gold, emeralds, rare things of value will be found within your borders. Textiles and fabrics from Medellin will rival anything in the world! New engineering techniques and computer technology and programs will amaze the world. Many nations will say where did these people come from and how did they develop such complex, yet simple and easy to understand systems? It will mostly be My dedicated believers that I will use in these areas and already it has started to happen. Don't forget to give Me the praise and glory and don't be corrupted by the wealth in your hands. Use the wealth wisely for the spread of the gospel. Don't be like other nations and forget it it I Who gives you the power to obtain wealth. Deut. 8:18

Yes, there are some elements of corruption in your government, but I will expose and remove it. You will largely not be affected by the chaos coming to most of the countries and governments of Latin America, as I destroy that root of communism and corruption in governments. Some nations in Latin America I will totally turn upside down, for I have heard a huge, united voice lifted up in prayer for many years against evil in governments and false religions. I AM breaking the yoke of witchcraft off your nation and it has started first in in Cali, Cartagena, Barranquilla, and will spread to the other places. I AM breaking that spirit of divination off this land! I will also move in these places and do a quick work. A new, mighty move of God is coming, so prepare your hearts to receive. It will totally transform your nation and for days at a time all commerce, schools, etc will almost stop, and a glory cloud of My presence will rest over that part of the nation. Then it will move to another part of the nation until it touches every segment of society. Some in high positions shall try to stop it, but they will be totally undone and down on their knees weeping before Me. The rich and poor, the proud and humble will all be under that cloud. The sinner will repent, the sick healed, demons will flee. It will be amazing to behold and to be involved in.

You are a people of destiny and you will fulfill your call. You will not be a goat nation but will be numbered among the blessed nations because of the prayers and dedication of the remnant people, who have cried night and day for the changes to come. Always remember the Jews and Israel in the days ahead, as many nations turn against them. Really stand with them for their full possession of all their land that God promised to Abraham. Pray for the peace of Jerusalem and that it would not be divided. Be faithful unto Me for I AM coming soon in all My power and glory.

Revival – Europe

July 08, 2013

Pockets of revival springing up in Europe. Pockets of revival springing up in the UK. Pockets of revival springing up in the Netherlands, also known as Holland to many people. Yes, I shall shake Holland in these days. I shall shake The Hague. I shall disturb their power that they think they have. They think they are a god unto themselves – The Hague Court. But I shall stir up that country. Yes, I AM stirring already. Already I AM pushing back the forces of evil in the Netherlands. Because where sin abounds, grace does much more abound. Romans 5:20 So how far they go with me depends on them: how far they are willing to give their lives totally unto Me. So it depends on the people and how far they want to go with Me in the Netherlands. Because I AM willing to go all the way with them. I AM willing to totally deliver them. I shall move in Belgium and don't be surprised – I shall even move in France. There shall be a move of God. And remember that bright light, it shall shine out of Bern, Switzerland. For the Lord says I shall move greatly in Bern, Switzerland. And in Geneva, in the Hague. In these places of world power. For the enemy would like to try to bring about and push his agenda. But those are the places I shall move says the Spirit of Grace. For this is a different season. This is a different time. For I shall do a quick work and there shall be pockets of revival all across Europe. Yes, the evil one is coming, but I shall have a brief move of My Spirit and it depends on the people and how hungry they are for Me. But yes, I have had a remnant people in Europe that's cried out to Me. And I shall even send missionaries into Europe from Africa. It shall be reverse missionaries. And some of these people that shall come from Africa as missionaries are people that were once Muslims. So there shall be a move of God among the Muslims in Europe and then many will go back to the Muslim countries. But the Lord says I shall have a quick work and a short work in Europe and then the evil one shall come on the scene, says the Spirit of the Lord, unto you.

Word From God – UK – Royal Family

July 2013

When Prince George was born, the Holy Spirit spoke to me and said his life would not be normal. I heard the word, "tragedy." Then, the Lord Jesus spoke to me of family sins revisited to sons and daughters. Sin has consequences! Your treatment of Jewish people has consequences according to the

Holy Bible. Remember Pharoah, who in the time of Moses, lost his firstborn son. Just as Pharoah's heart was hardened, so is the British government's heart hardened against God and His chosen people, Israel.

For years the Royal Family and the aristocrats have been involved in the occult and other evil works. Now, with the abomination of homosexual marriage in the UK, God says they have crossed the line. God is saying He is going to shake and then turn the government and the Royal Family upside down!

London Bridge Is Falling Down

December 05, 2013

London Bridge is falling down. London Bridge is falling down. The Tower of London is falling. London exposed. The government of David Cameron is exposed and turned upside down. The Royal Family dealt with. The country as a whole dealt with by Me. The Lord says yes, I shall move in London. I shall move in the UK once again, says the Lord thy God. The Lord says, I shall move. There is great wickedness in London, but I shall save London. The enemy would like to destroy London. The enemy would like for the Muslims to take over London and England itself. But the Lord says, I shall remove them before they can grab power. For they intend to grab power, but I shall totally expose their plans. The Lord says I shall expel them from the country. The Lord says a great move of God is coming to London and all the UK and Ireland and Northern Ireland. A great move of God such as the country has never seen before. Even greater than before. And the Lord says because of the prayers of the saints from old, because of the covenant I made with the old saints in past ages, because of the English people that are praying now, the Scottish people that are praying now, the Irish people that are praying now, the remnant people, the ragged, remnant people, that have been run ragged by the enemy, the Lord says, yes, the ones who are really praying the most because they have the numbers are the ones from India, the ones from Africa and the ones from Asia.

Yes these people who were under the British Empire and who have come in to the UK, yes, they are praying. I have a remnant people, a large, remnant people from those races and they are raising up a standard against the enemy. They are saying and are reminding God in their prayers, the UK brought the gospel to us! Don't let it go down! The UK brought the gospel to us and now we know and now we know and it's our time to stand with the UK so that it doesn't fall.

And the Lord says, I shall redeem the UK. I shall redeem them, whether they want to be redeemed or not. I shall redeem them. For the Tower of London, secularism – human secularism – corrupt finances – The Lord says I AM bringing down many Towers of London. I AM bringing down the Secret Societies. I AM bringing down the plans for One World Government from the UK. I AM bringing down their plots.

The Royal Institute. The ones that are trying to bring about the One World Government. The ones that would come against Me in the Universities. I AM bringing them down. I AM bringing down their strongholds. I AM bringing them down.

So the Lord says, I AM redeeming the time because of the evil days thereof. Yes, I AM going to turn that evil nation upside down. I AM going to bring it back financially again. I AM going to bring it back financially again, says the Lord thy God. So that they may go around the world and spread the gospel. And the Lord says, I will deal with the Muslims in that country. If they won't listen to the gospel, and if they won't repent, then I will move them out. I will expose them and move them out. I AM going to expose many terrorists' plots in the days ahead. I AM going to expose many other plots against the government. The Lord says I AM going to totally turn the government upside down and shake it out and then turn it all around, and the Royal Family, too, says the Spirit of Grace. The Lord says, they'll go to the nations once again and the Lord says, I shall use the UK mightily, once again. So the Lord says, yes, I shall move and then I will come says the Spirit of Grace.

Africa

May 02, 2014

Africa has been called "The Dark Continent." But the Lord

says, yes, in the days ahead, the Africans on this continent shall surely have their time. For I AM getting ready to raise up many African nations in this time. For oh, it's been called "The Dark Continent." Oh, there's been much darkness. Not only in skin color, but in witchcraft. In Satan worship. In the worship of demons and devils. But the Lord says, I AM getting ready to set many of the captives free. And even as I've told you before, I shall bring many to Philadelphia. Some shall have sandals. Some shall not have even shoes. Some shall have on only just robes and shall have strange dress and strange manners. But I shall bring them to Philadelphia. And I shall send many back to their own land. For I shall have a great move of God in Africa, says the Lord thy God. Oh yes, it shall be tremendous. And even the economies of those countries shall start to come up in many areas.

And the Lord says, I shall remove the evil and the curse over that land and I shall bring up many to be very wealthy people in the days ahead. I shall send them to the nations. I shall, in particular, send them to Europe, says the Lord thy God. For they shall go to Europe and take the gospel to that place and oh, it shall be a reverse of the way that it was years ago. For the Europeans came down from the Netherlands, from England, from Germany, and from many other lands and from Scandinavia, to Africa. But I shall send the Africans back to Europe to minister. And the Lord says I shall move and I'm moving now. And I shall right many wrongs in that land. I'm moving in Nigeria. I shall move in a mighty way in

South Africa and root out the Communists in that great land. For that's a prosperous land, but I must root out the Communists in that land. I shall move in Angola. I shall move in Kenya. There shall be a mighty move of God in Kenya. The Lord says, yes, in Malawi. In Mozambique, I shall move once again. And the Lord says, yes, even up in the desert, in Libya. I shall move in Sudan. I shall move the Arabs and the Muslims out of that land. I shall have a move of God in Sudan. Oh, yes, it shall be great. Many seeds have been planted there and I shall move there. And I shall move in Ethiopia one more time. And then they will figure in to some End Time Events. The Lord says I shall move in many different lands. And you shall see them coming to Philadelphia. You shall see them coming! They shall hear and learn of Me at your feet and at the feet of others. Then they shall go back to their countries. And then to many nations. Yes, I shall raise up a spirit of prophecy over that country. Many shall be prophets over that land. And yes, Madagascar, I shall move there. Yes, I shall move across that continent. And the Lord says, yes, I shall do a quick work, and you shall be surprised at how they even develop so quickly economically in the days ahead. For I have a remnant people who have been praying in that land. I have a remnant people that have for many years stood in the gap for Africa. So you shall see, they shall have their time and they shall have their influence on the nations. And they shall be a great influence on the Blacks in this great United States. The Lord says they shall be an influence. They shall be a bridge between the Whites and the Blacks in this country. I shall use them to be a bridge between the Whites and the Blacks in this country. I shall use them to have a great influence on this country. Even as the United States has influenced them from being missionaries in past generations, they shall have a dynamic influence on the United States and shall transform much of this society in many ways that you cannot even imagine. For the Lord says, yes, they will bring a light into this country. For when they really turn to Me, they shall turn wholeheartedly. And they shall not consider anything. They shall only consider Me.

So the Lord says I've heard their cry. I've heard their voice out of the darkness as they cried in the night time. I heard their voice. And the demons shall surely flee. Out of Africa the demons shall flee and into other lands out from that country. For they shall have their time finished in Africa. They shall flee to other nations in other parts of the world out of Africa. They shall be gone forever, says the Spirit of Grace unto you.

The Caribbean

June 23, 2014

There's a mighty tempest, the Lord says, building in the Caribbean. Oh, the ocean, waves are swelling. The winds are blowing. Hurricane type winds shall soon blow in the Caribbean. The ground shall shake in the islands. Much shaking shall go on. The Lord says, yes, I have a remnant people. I have a praying people in the Caribbean. They have been believing Me for the move of God. I have a people in Jamaica. I have a people in Guyana. I have a people in Suriname. In Grenada. In The Grenadines. In St. Lucia. In all the island nations. St. Kitt. St. Vincent. I have a people that have been praying. Trinidad and Tobago. I have a people in the island nations that have been praying. That have been seeking My face in the Caribbean. And, yes, a great storm is arising. A great tempest is in the ocean and shall be coming. The land shall be shaking. But the Lord says, I shall move after this happens. After the tempest, after the earth shaking, I shall move in those island nations. And I shall forever drive the voodoo spirit out of Haiti. I shall divide and conquer in the Caribbean, says the Lord thy God. I shall drive out the demon forces that have held those islands in bondage and in poverty. And I shall release the captives there and set them free. In the Dominican Republic, I shall move. I shall even move the Communists out of Cuba. For you shall see My Holy Spirit shall descend on the whole Caribbean Island nations and there shall be such a move of God. I shall sweep many into the Kingdom of God in the Caribbean. And many from the Caribbean shall be missionaries to Europe and to the United States and to the uttermost parts of the earth.

For I haven't forgot about the Caribbean people. I haven't forgot about My faithful remnant people in those island nations who have prayed and sought My face. The Lord says, this is their time. This is their season to rise up out of poverty. To rise up out of the demonic control that have held their families in bondage for many generations. This is the time when I shall truly move and shall set the captives free. And the Lord says a great surge of the Holy Spirit shall come to that whole area. So the Lord says watch and wait what I shall do, for great it shall surely be. And grand My plans are for those peoples. Many peoples there. Many island nations. They're crying out to Me. They're seeking Me.

So, yes. A great turmoil. A great shaking in the oceans. A great shaking on the land. But truly after this, I shall move and the Lord says, I AM with these people and they have My favor. I've heard their prayers and soon I shall answer, says the Spirit of the Lord unto you.

Europe

July 01, 2014

The Lord says, I shall move all throughout Europe in the days ahead. There shall be a turning to Me, but it shall be short lived, for many will turn back to the enemy as the Anti-Christ comes on the scene. But I have a people. Oh, yes, I shall move in the Scandinavian countries. I shall up end Iceland. I shall bring about new leadership there. For I have a remant there. I have a remnant people in Sweden. I shall have a move in Sweden. And I shall move there. I shall move in Denmark and Norway to a lesser degree, but Sweden, how sweet it shall be!

And the Lord says yes, I shall move in Finland. I shall protect Finland, yes, there's been a remnant people, there's been a group that has stood by and watched what has happened to their country, but they could not abide. So the Lord says I will rescue Finland in the days ahead. And even their Prime Minister, I shall remove him. For the Lord says, I'm not pleased. And I shall raise up a Daniel. I shall raise up a Joseph. I have a man that I shall raise up in Finland. And the Lord says, touch not Mine anointed and do My prophets no harm. For I shall use Finland for many Christians to escape out of Europe and the Scandanavian countries. I shall use Finland that many Jewish people might escape out of Europe in the days ahead. For the Lord says, I shall raise up a standard against the enemy in Finland. And the Lord says, there shall be a great move of God in Lithuania. In Latvia, which will even go into Poland and other of the Eastern European countries. I shall move but it shall be more limited in Estonia. But the Lord says, I shall move in the Scandinavian countries, for yes, they have cried out to Me. Yes, many shall turn back to the beggarly elements of this world and shall go the other way. But the Lord says yes, soon the time shall be ripe for Me to move in the Scandinavians countries, so Finland, be free! Scandinavia, be free! For I shall surely visit you in the days ahead. And I AM coming soon! So look for Me for I AM coming soon in all My glory and power says the Lord unto thee.

CHAPTER 3
PROPHECY CITIES-STATES-SCHOOLS

Move of God

March 08, 2012

Continue to seek My face for the great move of the God, the Great Awakening that I've been preparing you for is even at hand, says the Lord. So rejoice! Even before it starts. Continue to seek My face for the Great move of God, the Great Awakening that I've been preparing you for it is even at hand, says the Lord. So rejoice even before it starts! Give Me praise even before it starts. For I shall surely transform this place, this city, this area, this Nation. I shall truly do it and it shall start here, says the Lord God.

My Fire

March 08, 2012

I will do it.

You've been faithful to be gathered here two and three in My Name.

I will do it. I will do it. It only takes a little to get the fire going. Oh, yes, the fire is starting to burn brighter and brighter and brighter in this area of the country. And it shall spread. It shall spread to the nations. It shall spread to the other states. To the Capital. It shall spread to the nations. Oh, it shall spread. This is the time. This is the end time move of God that you've heard about. That you've talked about. It's even at hand. It's even at hand. It's even at hand. Oh, watch it spring up out on the Main Line. Watch it spring up in the worst areas of Philadelphia. Watch it spring up in Harrisburg. Watch it spring up all across this whole state. Watch it go down to Delaware. Watch it go up to New York and Boston. Oh and down to Washington and Richmond. Oh, watch it go! Watch it go! Watch it go! Oh, where the Holy Ghost goes nobody knows. It shall flow like a river. It shall like the lava from the volcano. It shall flow and cover – oh, it shall cover. And some will see it as a destructive force, but you know it as the blessed hope.

Yes, the evil one. He shall try to stop it, but he will not be able to.

Man will try to stop it, but he cannot. Government shall try to stop it. Schools shall try to stop it. Oh, but they cannot stop it. They cannot stop what I'm doing. Oh they cannot tone it down. They cannot stop it from TV. They cannot stop it from the books that will be written about it. They cannot stop what I'm doing, for it's a history breaking time.

In the midst of war and desolation and famine and distress, I shall move. I shall move and the people shall be ready for

Me. For they've been a hard hearted people. They have seared their consciences in this country, but I'll get to them! I'll get to them. I'll get to them. Oh, yes, they'll be down on their knees before Me. I know how to bring them down on their knees. I know how to bring this country down on its knees. And I shall do it, because they've hardened their hearts against Me – and it's going to take something to bring them down on their knees. But I will do it. It's going to take some destruction. It's going to take some distress. It's going to take some torment. It's going to take some things bad happening to bring them down on their knees, but I'll bring them down on their knees. I'll bring them down on their knees. I will bring this country down on its knees before Me.

Because I desire yet one more time to move in this great nation. I desire for this nation one more time to go out to the other nations. So you shall see, before it gets better in this country, in many areas it's going to get worse. It's going to get worse economically. It's going to get worse spiritually. It's going to get worse with earthquakes and tornadoes and distress and economically. In many ways it's going to get worse before it gets better. When the people cry out to Me that they've had enough – I will move in their midst. And I will have a great move of God. I'll have a great move of God. I'll set the captive free. I'll set the captive free, says the Lord.

Some Things Which Are To Come!
Prophecy New York City

November 14, 2012

(Secrets revealed to My Remnant People)

This is a season, a time when I will reveal Myself, who I AM, and there shall be a great leap into the supernatural as revelation knowledge of My ways are discovered in the Word. As they have eyes to see and ears to hear what the Spirit will say and instruct in these last days. There shall be an unveiling of My plans for these uncommon days. It is rare that one would even experience even one of these events in a lifetime, but you will experience earth shaking events that will cause the world at large to walk in fear. Know My children that you are safe under My wings, where you will abide.

San Francisco and New York City are an abomination to Me, as they have crossed the line. There shall be a great shaking in both cities. New York City will seem for a while to recover, but it will never fully recover itself until another disaster, calamity or great misfortune shall befall it. Great devastation, fire and days of rage shall fill that place. Pestilence shall be in her streets. The city with the Babylon spirit shall no longer be what it once was. Nations shall be in distress as they witness this mighty upheaval. Yes, I will move the United Nations off its foundation. Do these nations and peoples full of rage think they can overthrow Me? Do they think they can do harm to the Body of Christ and the Apple of My Eye,

Israel, and continue on day after day with their plots of evil? I shall bring down the towers of Babel and the goddess will be removed from her pedestal. Yes, the hedge of her protection was removed when leadership of this nation let their desire be known to pervert marriage. They prevented what I told man to do with their sexual sin and abortions.

I told them to reproduce and fill the earth with laughter of many children. They sought to steal My happiness. Their movement of sodomy started in New York and I will start to deal with it here. The nations shall tremble as they see My awesome power. I shall start in Washington and begin to deal there with the government. I will sweep through every government agency. I AM not with this Republic at this time. The parties and their plans mean nothing to Me at this time. I AM not with the Pentagon. These great warriors who command large numbers of men are so weak they would not stand up against this evil of sodomy. So I AM starting with the generals and admirals and I will go down the ranks. Now you shall see a season of defeat on the battlefields and in the oceans. Their plans, strategy, equipment shall fail them.

For a season, they will have one disaster after another. Everything will be a misstep and even they shall seem confused in the news report statements. World events shall surprise and overcome their calm demeanor. Yes, nuclear war is coming, but soon those weapons will be obsolete as a new weapon is almost ready which is 100% more powerful than atomic weapons. There is a surprise coming to the world as new sophisticated weapons come out of Israel. Soon the balance of military power will be changed in the world. Great days of war and conflict are yet to arrive and destruction as the world has never known. All these things must come to pass, but this I AM, the Great Holy God, I AM. No one else is like unto Me. These are days when I shall show My awesome power for all the world to see. I AM coming soon for a people who watch and wait for Me. My beloved, remnant people.

Prophecy for Michigan – Detroit

January, 2013

The M in Michigan stands for Mighty, Motors, and Music. For there shall be a mighty move of God across this state. A move of God such as has never been there. A mighty windstorm of My Holy Spirit moving in from Canada, crossing over Lake Huron from Windsor, Canada. Canada, you are Mine!

I shall start in Detroit with My Holy Spirit fire, which will burn for days and months upon end (Acts 2). Many have, but, no, I have not given up on this city, but I shall renew it! My fire shall first move to deal with that religious spirit which has corrupted that city, even into the government. Massive fraud, deceit, wickedness in churches and government, I will expose. I will no longer tolerate what the religious have done to My special city. I will move in music and a new sound will come to the front that will set the captive free. I started a distinct sound in the 60s, but it was high-jacked by the enemy. I raised up whole industries to finance the gospel, but the spirit of greed stole My ideas and corrupted them. Everything was done to the extreme and excess.

Detroit shall once again be the motor and music city, but more than that, it shall be a "My Movement" city. Revival in the spiritual, political and in industry. I shall bring renewal and it shall be better than before. Music, yes My music shall go to the nations and break yokes of bondage and bring in healing and a cure. Many shall be healed as they listen to the sounds and the words.

Yes, Grand Rapids shall come forth! This is your time to rise and fulfill your destiny. I will bless you because of the praying remnant people who have prayed and waited before Me and took a stand against that old fox who wanted to destroy the state.

Lansing, how I do weep for you and all your corruption and racism, but I shall break the strongholds there and bring you up in status and deliver the ones there in bondage. In this time I will expose the corruption in the unions and the deceit in the motor industry. Yes, I shall melt the gold in Michigan and take out all the impurity and use this rich land in the days ahead.

The real purpose of all the M's in Michigan is the M which is your purpose and destiny: Missions! I will send many from Michigan to missions around the world and use your money to finance My end time move. My Holy Spirit will motivate you to move out in faith. Yes, the enemy will no longer have you. Michigan, you are Mine! You are My prized apple!

Prophecy for Philadelphia

January 09, 2013.
Sung while Butch Stockton plays keyboard.

Philadelphia! Philadelphia! Hold on to your hat, for I AM coming in all My glory to sweep you off your feet, even as I weep for you, My City of Brotherly Love!

I will restore, redeem and bring you forth better than in the first. Build. Restore. Refurbish. Purchase Land and Property, for My city shall be great in the end time days! Hotels built. Airports expanded. And housing everywhere redeemed. Get ready for a flood of people to come from the East, Far East, Middle East. From everywhere under My sun. A great flood. A great mass of people who have heard of Me and My excellent ways. My balm of healing for the nations. Look, Listen and See for they are coming - every race, tribe, tongue, nation. Yes! An amazing move of My Holy Spirit in power and great demonstration. A great spiritual awakening shall start here in My covenant city and will go around the world. My Name and the name of My beautiful city shall be on everyone's lips, as they speak in awe and respect of My Glory.

Yes, William Penn, your love of Me and our covenant of

this land shall be known far and wide. I shall have My way in this time, and no man's systems, school, military, organization or religion shall be able to stop Me. This move shall help to usher in My soon coming; for behold, I come quickly and will not tarry. Look for Me!

Redeem the Time!

February 18, 2013

Redeem the time because of the evil days. (Ephesians 5:16) Time is running out. Time is speeding up. It is a race against time. The closer you get to an event happening, it seems like time speeds up. Yes, time is being shortened. You will see when it is ready to happen that the situation changes quickly, so fast that one can hardly keep up. Conditions affecting the event will feel like they are happening over night. After the new pope is set in his position, world events shall accelerate, one by one. There shall be more signs in the heavens and upon the earth. Earthquakes shall increase and all manner of unstable weather. Hot where it should be cool and cool where it should be warm. So just go with Me, rest in Me, for the most unrestrained, uncontrolled events will soon happen. Events shall seem shocking to the world at large, as they unfold, but not for My remnant people. For they will rejoice in these birth pains, as they will know this is the time they prayed for, waited for, longed to see.

Events will unfold and then suddenly a "Great Spiritual

Awakening" that will destroy national and international mindsets and set the captive free. I will expose evil lies that have kept nations in bondage for hundreds of years. Spiritual freedom such as has never been seen! Jesus Christ shall show all the world His power and glory! Then shall be a quick work that will destroy satan's kingdoms. And then, just as quickly, Jesus, our Savior, shall come in all His glory in the clouds. My saints, this is the time to work, for the time is coming when no man will be able to labor (John 9:4). The time is short, so redeem it (Ephesians 5:16). And, as you work, know that your labor of love is not in vain. (1 Corinthians 15:58) Time is running out, so run the race and receive the victor's crown, My precious ones.

The Beauty of His Holiness

Marc 11, 2013

Sung while Butch Stockson plays keyboard

Worship the Lord in the beauty of His holiness. Oh, My saints, walk in the beauty of His holiness. Walk upright before Me. I'm calling you into a holy place. I'm calling you into holiness. Oh, you must be holy, even as I AM holy. This I demand of thee. Be likening unto Me. I made you in My image. I created you to be as one with Me. I created you to walk upright, to fellowship with Me. Oh come up a little higher. Oh let Me purify you by My fire, My holy fire. I'm bringing you forth as vessels of honor unto Me. You're almost there – but you can take some more heat. I'm burning out all the dross out of you. Refining you. Purifying you. Making you pure as gold. So check your motives. Check your plans. Check your life against My word, I say unto thee. Check your life against My word. The beauty of His Holiness. Be holy, walk holy, even as I Am holy, says the Lord.

O, come unto Me all that are burdened and heavy laden. Lay your burdens at My feet. I Am calling unto thee, walk in the garden with Me. Enjoy the beauty of the garden. Come and fellowship with Me in the garden. We shall walk together in holy fellowship. This is a time to walk uprightly before Me – to walk in holiness before Me. Even as the world walks in more evil, and their ways become an abomination, their iniquity has caught My attention. But you, My precious ones, you're a different breed. I have made you in My image. I have created you in My image. So come a little higher. Come up above the confusion and the chaos that's coming. I'll suspend you above it all. I'll take you on a higher level, a higher plane. Come up into the heavens with Me. There's rest in the heavens, as you walk with Me. Walk on My clouds of glory. You're going to see My glory in the days ahead. You're going to be in My glory and caught up in the glory cloud. Even today, the glory is descending on thee, my saints. My dear hearts. Wait before Me. For the time is here. The time you have waited for is almost here. So anxiously await a little while longer for My coming. My Spirit's coming in all the earth. And I will come to earth one more time, says the Spirit of God. I'm going to come for one last great harvest. Wonderful shall it be. Many shall be caught up into the heavenlies. Help Me bring them in to the heavenlies. Help Me bring them into My kingdom. You will share in My victory.

Put in the sickle, for the harvest is ripe. Put in the sickle, for the last great harvest is ripe. This is the day that Joel spoke about. He is pouring out His Spirit on all mankind, so come forth, sons, come forth, daughters, and prophecy unto Me. This is what was written, so come unto Me. Come unto Me, all ye that are weary. Rest. Rest. Rest in Me. Sit at My feet, and learn of Me.

These are important days. These are the days when you'll really know Me. And as you walk with Me, you'll really know Me. You'll know My voice in the days ahead, as I say, Walk to the right, move to the left, go to the North, move to the south. My Holy Spirit winds will blow with thee. Keep My covenant. My Son, He established a new covenant. Walk in that covenant.

I'm coming. I'm coming into your midst with wave after wave of My glory. Soon you will see just a little and then more. Wave after wave of My glory coming in to Philadelphia. Wave after wave of My glory shall soon be sweeping over Philadelphia. Wave after wave of My glory. Yes, I AM coming to purify this place. This is special ground that was dedicated to Me. Philadelphia, you're Mine. Philadelphia, turn not away. I'm calling to you, as a Lover would call unto you, Philadelphia, come to My arms. I'll mend your wings. I'll smooth out your feathers. I'll bring a healing balm. The healing balm of Gilead shall be in your midst. Day after day, I will rest over Philadelphia. Day after day, My glory will be felt. Oh, it's coming soon, it's coming soon. Many peoples are coming to Philadelphia. Hear the sound of their feet as they come into Philadelphia. Hear them as they fly into Philadelphia. They're coming from distant lands, hungry for Me.

So weep for Me, Philadelphia. Weep over Philadelphia. Weep. Weep. Weep. Cry out for the lost. The lost are coming to Philadelphia. Now is the time to cry out for the lost, for their salvation, for their eyes to see. I'm bringing those that have been perplexed and those in distress. And the nations in distress, they shall see a glimmer of hope in Philadelphia. They shall see the Light upon the hill. My lighthouse. The Holy Spirit shall draw men to this port. Come on in by the ship loads. Ship loads of people coming from the nations to Philadelphia. That's the buzz word – Philadelphia, PA. Oh William Penn, your prayers shall be honored. Oh it was not an easy life, William Penn, but I'll honor your life. In the knowledge that you had you walked after me and I will honor that says the Lord. You would have longed to see this day, when I moved by My power and My grace, bringing every race, every tribe and every nation together as one, under My wings. A City of Brotherly Love, it shall truly be.

O look where are the crimes and the murders? They shall be gone. Where's the distress and the unrest? And the homeless? They shall be gone. Just caught up into My arms. O for

I will gather you. I longed to gather Jerusalem up under My wings, but they would not at that time come under My wings. Oh, but I rejoice because Philadelphia will come under My wings. Oh, you'll be under the wings of My protection in the days ahead. For there will be great danger in this land. There'll be great tests and trials in this land. Oh, City of Refuge, you just be quiet and still before Me. Oh, sweet City of Refuge, they're coming to find peace here. Wars and distress of nations. The waves of the oceans are raging. Oh, come unto Me all you weary and those that are heavy laden. Come to Philadelphia and find rest.

Top of The Mountain

March 11, 2013

Sung While Butch Stockton plays Keyboard.

Oh, the Lord says, I'm taking you to the top. I'm taking you to the top of the mountain. Oh, you're almost there. Do not be discouraged any longer. You'll not be downcast, oh, my soul. You're almost to the top. Oh, yes My children, I'm taking you to the top….. All the way to the top. I'm taking you to the top of the mountain. You'll be able to see very far. You'll realize the long road that you came down and that you came from. You'll not forget where you came from. You'll not forget the hard times and the past times. But I'm taking you into a new season on top of the mountain. You'll be able to look out into the future. Oh, the future is very bright! Oh, down below will be the destruction. Oh, down below will be the evil. But I'm taking you to the top of the mountain. At the very top is the pure, white snow. The glacier water to refresh you. The dry air. The dry air. Breathe it on in. Breathe it on in. For you're on My mountain top. Oh, breathe in all My glory. Breathe in all My abundance. See all the world below. I'm taking you to the top. By the power of The Holy Spirit, I'll bring you closer to Me on the mountain top. A mountain top experience. Oh, that's where you'll be.

Yes, rejoice today. My glory is settling, for I'm taking you to the top. Oh, that's where the provision is, on top of the mountain. That's where My glory is, on top of the mountain. That's where your health is, your provision; it's with Me. I've prepared a place before you in the presence of your enemies. Oh, look down the mountain – down at the bottom of the mountain. I'm taking you to the top. Oh, it's a new day that's dawning. Oh, see the sun glistening in the snow. Oh, at night see the moon upon the mountain top. Oh, it's where you belong. No more valleys down below. Just one peak after another peak. One mountain peak after another mountain peak. Now just peep from the mountain peak, and see into My glory realm. For this realm's all around you. It's a high altitude. Don't worry – they're just My glory clouds. Caught up in My glory clouds.

I'm going to keep you in the days ahead, up in My glory clouds. The days of misery are coming in the valley. But I'm going to keep you on the mountaintops. You'll be out of harm's way. You'll be out of the fires and the destruction that shall lay waste at noon time every day. A terrible time in the valley it shall be. Oh, it could have been a lush valley – but they gave it to the evil one in place of Me. So I'm taking My precious people on the mountaintop. For I'm the Soon Coming King. So wait for Me, and look for Me. Wait for Me on the highest mountain, My children, for soon I'm coming.

I'm coming in all My power and glory, so just abide with Me. Oh, let My words abide in Thee. Rest in peace and safety and security; it's assured for thee. The peace and safety in the days ahead, I say, it's assured for thee. Even though destruction lays waste at noon day, it shall not come nigh thee. But only My peace and victory, My security in the new covenant. Only that will keep you free. So ride the waves. Ride the waves of the glory clouds.

Caught up in the glory clouds. Wave after wave of My glory. Oh just be caught up in the glory cloud. In the days ahead, just be caught up in the glory clouds. There'll be some days – day after day – you'll just be caught up in the glory clouds; all day long and all week long, just in the glory cloud. Oh there's coming a precious time when you won't feel the pain around you. There'll be days and days of My visitation in Philadelphia. Days and days of My glory cloud, filling that place, til it can contain no more. So the glory will come and you'll give it out. Then I'll bring a little wave of people into Philadelphia. And I'll give out My glory to the nations. Receive My glory. Receive My glory clouds and then pass them on – give them out. As you pass them on, I'll bring another glory cloud your way. I'm preparing you to minister to the multitudes that will be coming your way. Oh, many strange tongues and many strange people they will send to thee. But they're My people that I desire to see set free.

Oh, I created them in My image, too. Oh, their hair, their dress, their style shall confound you and confuse.........But just accept them, with the open arms of Jesus. Watch them come into the Kingdom, even though their languages are strange and their customs are strange. But the Lord says, they're looking for Me. Remember how you felt when you found Me? These ones, dear hearts, are looking for Me, too.

I've sent them from a foreign land – so stay in the mountaintop experience with Me in the days ahead. Oh, not in the sinking sand. Don't go back to the sinking sand. Stay on the solid rock, Christ Jesus. High in the mountaintop. So breathe in the mountain air. Can't you feel the fresh breeze of the Holy Spirit? It's gently blowing on the mountaintop. The fresh, cool breeze of the Holy Spirit. It's like the fragrance after the rain.

Oh, My saints, Jesus has a fragrance. When Jesus walks into your presence, He has a fragrance. Can't you smell the fragrance of Jesus Christ today? He's walking in your midst today. Oh, it's a fresh fragrance – it's not overpowering, but it's fresh, fresh as the new fallen snow. It's the fragrance of your Savior, your Lord and Savior, Jesus Christ. He's looking for a people. He's drawing a people unto Himself. He's drawing many unto Himself, from the nations. From the four corners of the earth they shall come to Philadelphia, the City of Brotherly Love.

My City of Provision, My City of Refuge, let the Jews rest before they go. Let the Jews rest before they go. Bless the Jews and speak peace over them before they go. Before they go to Israel, speak a blessing on the Jews. Oh, yes, they're going into the unknown. Some will even die for Me. Oh, bless these Jews. Many shall rise up and take the gospel to the nations. Many of these Jews will take the gospel back to the nations they came out of. They'll be My end time missionaries.

Taking the gospel of peace and salvation, oh, yes, to the Jew first and also to the Gentile. Oh, Romans 11 shall be fulfilled. I'm opening their eyes and they're going to look deep into the eyes of their Savior. They shall weep and howl and cry and pray, Oh Savior, take me in, Oh by the way, can I have a part in this ministry? And He'll say, come, walk with Me up to the mountain.

Bring them all up to the mountaintop. There's plenty of room at the mountaintop. So weep and cry today for the nations. The nations are in distress today. Weep and cry for their salvation, and the Soon Coming King of Kings. He's coming back soon. My saints, rest in this fact: He's coming soon. And He'll not tarry. But He's coming soon; oh, yes, in that glory cloud.

Now is the time to labor, for there is a time coming when

no man shall labor. Now is the time. The harvest is ripe. Soon you'll see them coming from the North, South, East and West; Middle East, Far East and every place under the sun. Oh they're coming by the multitudes, looking for their Lord and Savior, Jesus Christ: King of Kings and Lord of Lords, the Soon Coming King! He'll establish His Kingdom in this place, in this time, upon the earth. He will establish in Jerusalem. Look and see. Watch and wait. Be ready. Be ready. Be ready for Me.

I'm Shaking Philadelphia

March 20, 2013

A great day of shaking in Philadelphia.

It has started now. It has already started. I'm shaking that city. I'm shaking Philadelphia. I'm shaking the government. I'm shaking the economic foundation. Yes, I'm shaking the Masonic spirit out of that place. I'm shaking the mafia out of that place. Yes, a great shaking in Philadelphia.

The corruption shall be exposed. I shall expose, expose, expose evil thoughts and evil deeds done in Philadelphia. I shall expose it and many will be sent to prison, says the Lord thy God. Many will be brought down. I AM totally exposing the corruption in the school system, in the police department, in the fire department. I AM totally exposing great businesses that are corrupt there:

Comcast, I will deal with them. ATT, I will deal with

them. I AM exposing what UPS is doing, even in that city. I AM exposing the corruptness. Many who seem to be upright shall be exposed as behind many evil things. Yes, I will expose the Mummers. Yes, yes, yes, yes – their days are numbered. I AM totally going to clean that city before I move, says the Lord. This is the part. There was no repentance on the part of …….. or on the part of others in Philadelphia. There was no repentance in the government for their evil deeds or for their support of homosexual marriage; for their support of adultery; or for their support of abortion. I will expose ministries in the city considered great and infallible. I shall expose the evil. I shall expose it all, and then I will move by My spirit. I will fulfill My part of the covenant, even as Ben Franklin prayed. Even as he called for prayer at the constitutional convention.

I shall move in Washington and expose evil there. Even as Ben Franklin said, let's pray. Others would say in the capital of Washington, let's pray. In the Senate and the House, they'll say, let's pray, even as Ben Franklin gave the example years ago. So yes, I shall move in Washington, D.C. But first I shall start and expose in Philadelphia. For I will keep My covenant with William Penn. Oh, yes, I will surely fulfill all that I have promised in this city. And you will see up and down the East Coast - in Baltimore, in New York, in Boston - I shall expose the corruptness in the government. I shall shake the governments. I shall shake this whole region and I will have My way. For I will first start in Philadelphia and there shall be a great move of God coming in, coming in, coming in to Philadelphia from all the nations. Coming in, coming in, coming in - Many don't believe it shall happen. Even those who've heard that God's going to move in Philadelphia don't really believe it, but I shall shock them. And the ones who think that they would come in from the outside and have a part in this, they're robbers and thieves and liars. And I will have nothing to do with them. But I will raise up a remnant people in this city and I will raise up a remnant people and bring them to this city. And they're the ones that are unknown. They're the ones that I shall use to spark and to set ablaze this city for Me, says the Lord thy God.

Glory Cloud Over Philadelphia

March 27, 2013

You shall be truly amazed, day after day, of My people coming in here from the other nations. Day after day waves of glory, healing glory, deliverance glory. The glory cloud shall be over this city night and day. It shall be wave after wave of My glory and it shall sweep. Wave after wave of healing, shall sweep. There will be mass healings sweeping the city. Even when people hit the airport, they will be healed instantly. When they drive into the city limits, in the cars, they will be healed. They will come from every direction even in this country. Day after day when commerce, when school, when everything will stop because it shall be a day of My glory.

There shall be a glory cloud over this city. That glory cloud will even be a protection over this city from the bad weather and from enemy attacks. It will be that shield of the Holy Spirit that will be a protection over this city from lack, from want, from famine. It will be a wave of My glory sweeping over this city for many days. Day after day after day. There shall be such a protection over this whole area, says the Lord. Such a protection. And there shall be such a joy, such a peace, such a rest. The people won't even want to move. But after many days of being here in My glory, they will move back to their nations and they'll take the gospel with them. For I will train them up quick and I AM going to raise up laborers into the harvest. Fret not how it could be, for I have many laborers in this country and in the other nations that are mature Christians, and I will bring to raise up this new generation of Christians. And they will take the gospel back to their countries. Countries that have never even heard My name shall know Me. Countries that have hated Me will come to Me in a day's time, even in a week's time it will seem to you. But there will be mass conversions. For they shall put down their weapons of war and anger and come to Me. I shall change the hard hearts. I shall change their mindsets. I shall move in such a way that you could never imagine! The authorities shall be shaken up. Those that try to control things behind the scenes shall be shaken. Everybody will try to stop it, but no one shall be able to stop it. I shall stop them, says the Lord, thy God. I shall stop every government. I shall stop every institution that would try to come against My end days move of God. For I shall have My way in this hour. I shall have My way with the nations for they are Mine. For I have created these nations and these people, every tongue and tribe. I have created them and they are My people. And they will come to Me because I AM drawing them unto Myself, says the Lord thy God.

Intercede for Nations Philadelphia

March 27, 2013

These are the days of the miraculous. These are the days of the supernatural.

And the Lord says today, Oh, My little ones! Only believe! Only believe! All things are possible, only believe! Ask of Me for the heathen. Ask of Me for the heathen nations, and you shall have them, says the Lord thy God. Ask of Me. Ask largely that your joy may be fulfilled. Stand in the gap for these nations and these people. Nations! Nations! I need them into My kingdom! I desire them into My kingdom! My Son died for these nations. And so they're found wanting before Me. But intercede and stand in the gap for these nations. Many decisions are being made by many peoples and many nations. So even as My Holy Spirit calls them unto Me, stand in the gap. Will you be the watchman on the wall? Will you wait before Me in intercession and prayer? Wait before Me for these nations and nations and people and I shall bring them in. Yes, I will do a great work in this city. Yes, I will send them out from this city, after I have refined them. I shall bring them in and do a quick work. I shall burn out the dross in their lives and I shall send them back to their nations says the Lord thy God. So stand in the gap. Stand before Me in prayer for these people, for My hand is not shortened that I cannot save and cause a great deliverance, says the Lord thy God.

Philadelphia, You Are Mine!

March 27, 2013

You're Mine. You're Mine. I'll not let the enemy have you! Philadelphia, you are Mine! And I shall have you as a prized possession. As the apple even of My eye. I shall have you, My city on the hill. I shall have you by the sea. Philadelphia, you are Mine. And I shall truly, in the days ahead, shake this city by My power. I shall shake the government in this city. I shall shake the schools. I shall shake out all the corruption in the fire department, the police department, and the businesses. I shall shake out all the corruption, all the racism, and all the evil. I shall shake it out of this city. I shall turn this city and this area upside down and inside out in the days ahead. They shall be totally undone when I AM finished with them. They won't know right side up or which way to go, but the Lord says, then they'll go in My Holy Ghost flow, for I shall flow in this city. I shall flow in this city. And as I drive out the enemy, I shall raise up a standard and bring My

Spirit into this city without measure. I shall bring godly men and women into positions in churches. I shall bring My remnant people into the midst of you. I shall bring them up in the governments and in business. I shall raise up such a standard against the enemy in this city that it shall be an example to those around the world, and they will even come here and be in awe and amazement at the way I transform this city! Oh, yes, great it shall be! Think not how it could be; for I can do everything! And nothing is impossible with Me. So just only believe and see this place shaken up and delivered and the captives set free, says the Spirit of the Lord.

Pieces of A Puzzle

March 27, 2013

Puzzle. Puzzle. Pieces of a puzzle.

Concerning this ministry, the Lord is fitting all the pieces of the puzzle together. Even before, there were some pieces that wouldn't fit this puzzle, but that's because they were from a different puzzle. And so the Lord is even saying today that He is going to fit together all the pieces of the puzzle, concerning peoples, even concerning building locations of the future, concerning finances, concerning the personnel. He is going to fit all the pieces of the puzzle together and where it hasn't been clear in the future, it's going to be clear. It's going to be clear as all the puzzle pieces come together and work together. It's going to be a beautiful picture. There's going to be a beautiful panorama. There's going to be a beautiful thing coming out of this place. Even concerning each and every one here, other than this ministry; the other ministries represented in this place, the other businesses represented in this place; yes, all the pieces of puzzle of your lives are going to fit together. The family members that you have prayed for – they're going to come into the Kingdom of God. For I have promised you and your whole household that they would be saved. Acts 16:31 And you have been faithful to be gathered here: one, two, three, four, five. You have gathered here in My name, and I'm going to remember all those prayers and I'm going to save your household. I'm going to redeem your households and your families – so don't be in fear or dread that they'll be lost. Don't be in dread or fear concerning your finances and even the things that I'm calling you to do. For the pieces of the puzzle are going to fit together in the days ahead and it will become very clear, even when the puzzle is half way finished, it will become evident the way I'm going. For I AM moving in this time in a mighty way. I'm going to fit together the puzzle of Philadelphia. I'm going to put all the players on the board. Even right now, I'm looking at this map on this wall here and it is just plain – just like a puzzle. And all the pieces of all the nations are all right near on this table. We're going to take all these nations, we're going to take cities and we're going to start putting them on this map. And the Lord is going to show us one by one who the players shall be and how the pieces of the puzzle shall fit together.

And the Lord says, Nations and nations are weighed in the balances and found wanting. You will know in the days ahead who will be the sheep nations and who will be the goat nations. And some are in the valley of decision now. They could be a goat nation or they could be a sheep nation. But I AM going to take this puzzle and put it together and as you pray; and as you take this map here, in the days ahead, as you pray, I will lead you to pray. And as you put your hands on the different flags that represent the nations and as you put your finger on the map where these nations are located, for days at a time, I will tell you to pray for this nation and that nation. And you will see them shift back and forth. And one week, you'll pray and they'll be aligned with the goat nations. The next week, they'll be aligned with the sheep nations. And so their destinies will be fulfilled and you'll bring many into the sheep nations as you pray in here. For think it not strange, I'm going to bring strange people in your midst. And I will raise up houses of prayer in the Philadelphia Area. But I will raise up one central House of Prayer says the Spirit of the Lord, where there will be at least 100 praying there 24 hours a day. Sometimes, there'll be 1, 2, 300 people praying in that place. And it's a nice place, too, says the Lord. And it's a blessing, says the Lord. There'll be much healing. There'll be much ministry in that place. But there's going to be several places where there'll be Houses Of Prayer and Schools of the Prophets that I will raise up, but there will be one central main location where the Spirit of God will really move and there will be the glory cloud hanging in that place. And I will bring it all together. And it will fit together like pieces of a puzzle. And you will see the people coming from the nations. Some of them will even smell bad. Some of them will look bad. Some of them will seem very strange and different to you and will have strange customs. But don't push them away, don't be stand-offish with them, but take them into your arms and welcome them. For some very unlovely people will come across your pathway from the desert, people from the jungles, people who are even barefooted, people who you don't understand, people with strange ways and strange looks. They will come here, but I AM bringing them from all around the world to Philadelphia. I'm bringing them to these prayer rooms. I'm bringing them to this city. They shall come here and learn of me at your feet. They shall know of Me. And they shall go back to their nations. So welcome these strangers in your midst, for some of them could even be angels that you will be entertaining. So welcome these strangers in your midst in the days ahead, for I AM bringing them far and wide and near, from the North, South, East, and West. All the nations are going to come to this city, and I shall truly establish a great work; so in the days ahead you will see all the prophecies and all the words I have given you. You will see them be like the pieces of a puzzle and one by one you will see the puzzle and you will start to get the bigger picture of what I AM going to do. I AM going to fit together this puzzle for Philadelphia. I AM going to fit together this puzzle for this ministry, says the

Lord. All the pieces are going to come together. And it shall be a great time and it shall be a great victory, and you will see how it will all work together. Everything is going to work together for My good, says the Spirit of the Lord.

The Day of The Lord

April 04, 2013

The Lord would say the Day of the Lord is even at hand. Joel 2:1

The Day of the Lord is even at hand. So rejoice at what I AM doing!

Rejoice at the great days ahead. For the Day of the Lord is even at hand and who can stand against the hand of the Lord? What man? What person? What organization can stand against Me? For this is the time and the season when I shall have My way in all the earth. For the Day of the Lord is approaching! Can't you see that the Day of the Lord is almost here? So the Lord says today you must cry out for the lost and dying in every area of the world. You must cry out for the lost and dying. And yes, I will start with that Great Spiritual Awakening in this City of Philadelphia. I will start and it will spread to the left and to the right, and to the North and to the South and to the East and to the West, and to the four corners of the earth. And the four winds of the earth shall carry it to every dry and parched land. For there are many dry and parched lands around the world where they have never heard of Me, and where they have never heard of the Gospel of Jesus Christ or how He can set the captive free.

So, yes, I'll set the captives free in the days ahead. Oh, a great explosion of the Holy Spirit shall surely be, such as the world has never seen! Many saints of old dreamed to see such a day, but you shall be in the middle of everything, says the Lord. As you continue on your face before Me crying out for the lost, you must spend more time, I say, crying out for the lost and dying. And I will bring them to you. I will bring the nations to you. And they will even dwell for a time amongst you, until I send them back to their nations. Oh, so prepare for the mighty harvest. Prepare yourselves spiritually and mentally and physically. Prepare yourselves for long hours in the days ahead. There shall be joy in the house, but there shall be long days when you will spend many hours with many different kinds of people that you know not their customs, or anything about them. But I will prepare your hearts to receive the lost. For the lost and dying shall come to this place and be delivered and set free, says the Lord thy God.

Time of The Harvest

April 13, 2013

This is the time of the harvest. Some would say that it is 6 months or longer, then the harvest. But I say unto you, My precious ones today, this is the season of the harvest. It is almost upon you, so prepare for the harvest, for it shall be great.

Oh, yes, I shall redeem those places that I called for My places. Those schools that I have called for My places. Yes, the Ivy League schools; yes, even Princeton, Harvard, Yale and those schools that I raised up to be a voice – My Voice to the nations. Yes, I will redeem them. I will expose all the evil there in that place. And I will remove those behind the evil. All those that have come against Me and My people. I will remove them from their lofty positions. I will remove that spirit of intellect from that place. And I will bring the Holy Spirit into that place, says the Lord. For a great revival it shall surely be. It shall start in the Ivy League schools and go all the way down to even the community colleges. But I will have My way in this great land. For this is the time of the harvest. This is the time and the season. It is almost upon you. Soon, there shall be great wars. Soon, there shall be great destruction around the earth, in several different places. And then you shall see the start of a world-wide move of God. Great it shall surely be! It shall be the Kingdom move of God. It shall the be the Kingdom move with signs and wonders and I shall show Myself strong, even in the heavenliest with signs and wonders, even in the heavenliest . Mass healings! Many people raised from the dead and, yes, the blind eyes shall surely see. Yes, you shall see the heathen coming into Me, into My kingdom, into My place that I have prepared for them. So great shall be the harvest. Thrust in the sickle. Prepare your hearts to receive the unlovely. Prepare your hearts to receive even the ugly. Those that you would not even want to be associated with. Prepare your heart to receive many different kinds of people, for all kinds of people shall come into My kingdom. For My heart is for all the people in the earth, that not one would be lost but that all would come into the saving knowledge of Jesus Christ. So work while you can for the time is short and then I will truly come once again.

The Great Visitation

June 03, 2013

The time of the visitation is even at hand. All the things I have told you about for one, two or three years, the time is even at hand. This is the time of the Great Visitation that I've told you about. It shall be overpowering. It shall be overwhelming. Many shall be overwhelmed at their jobs; when they're driving; in their homes, in the schools. This is the time when I shall overwhelm this city by the presence and the power and the deliverance of the Holy Spirit, and they shall be weeping in the supermarkets. They shall be weeping in the schools. Yes, it shall be uncontrollable. Weeping before Me. And no man, no institution, no government, nothing shall be able to stop the sweep of My Holy Spirit. So I shall sweep out Philadelphia. I shall sweep out the evil, and truly I shall have My way in this time. So prepare your hearts to receive and accept the new thing that I will do in this hour. For first there must be a great shaking. There must be a great shaking and then I will move, says the Spirit of Grace unto you.

Suddenlies

June 03, 2013

I spoke to you several months ago and said it would be two, three months and then there would be many suddenlies. This is the time I spoke of. It is even at hand when you shall see many more suddenlies. This is time of the great destruction and the great war I told you about. This is the time when the move of God shall truly start. Not six months and then the harvest, but now. The harvest is even before you. The many things I have told you that would soon come upon the earth economically, politically, spiritually. The time is even at hand. You are at the cusp. You are at the beginning. You are at the tipping point, as it were, when many things shall happen in the days ahead. You're in the very beginnings of what shall soon happen in all the earth. Be not in fear. Be not in dread, but be in excitement as you see how I will move suddenly. There'll be many suddenlies in the days ahead. Many suddenlies how I shall change your individual lives and your corporate life. How I shall change the life of the Body of Christ or how I shall change the life of the Jewish people. Even the Arab as I reach them in this time. And even the Muslim as I reach them in this time. For there shall be many suddenlies.

Yes, there's a great shaking coming to Philadelphia. It shall start here and go around the world. I'm going to deal with those who have tried to stop the move of the Holy Spirit and the ones who have tried to bring evil into Philadelphia. I shall truly move and the Lord says, yes, suddenly, a great shout. A great voice of an angel from heaven. And that angel shall even come down and shall blow a trumpet over Philadelphia. For the time is even at hand when I will send that angel down to blow that huge trumpet over Philadelphia. It shall be the horn that shall cause many to come unto Me. The sound of the trumpet of God shall soon blow over Philadelphia. So watch and wait for Me, for soon you shall see the signs and wonders and miracles. You shall see the people running after Me in this great city and in this land, says the Spirit of Grace.

Pillows of Rest

June 06, 2013

Yes, for those who watch and wait and seek My face, I shall make you pillows that many shall rest their heads on in the days ahead. You shall be as bright as stars, shining bright like a star into the darkness. For the days ahead they are even UPON (great emphasis on ON) you. The days of darkness and turmoil. For it shall be a time more dark than World War I and World War II. It shall be a time of great distress and darkness and destruction upon the earth. But you, My Precious Ones, who have My heart and know My voice, you shall lead and guide many in the days ahead. Many shall rely on you and the strength I have imparted into you. For truly it shall be a difficult time; oh, yes, even for My saints that I have raised up by the Most High God. Truly it shall be a difficult time in the days ahead, but you shall lead many into safety. You shall lead many into salvation. You shall lead many into deliverance in the natural as well as the spiritual. But it shall be a difficult time. But fear not don't, dread it, for it must come. Oh, yes, even as the days of darkness come, after that the light, the glorious light shall shine, and My Word shall go forth around the world. It shall be the great move of God that you are looking for. But, first, before the great move of God comes in its fullness, shall be many difficult, dark days. But you shall be My guiding light to many people. For even in the church they will look to you, for many will not endure sound doctrine at this time. Many will be running to and fro - uncertain and afraid and in fear because they have not prepared. They have not kept their lamps trimmed. Oh, keep your lamps trimmed. Keep your supply of oil – the Holy Spirit's oil in your lamps. And you will not be put to shame in the days ahead. For many in the Body of Christ will be put to shame, for they have not prepared their hearts and minds or even their spirits for that which is come. But you, My Precious Saints who gather before Me, you have prepared for the time is even at hand. It is UPON (emphasis on ON) you and now it shall suddenly come, says the Spirit of the Lord.

The Jews

July 07, 2013

The Jews. I shall move in the midst of the Jews worldwide. Yes, I shall move among the Jews in this country. There are many in the Philadelphia area and I shall move in the midst of the Jews. I shall start more and more every day to open the eyes of their understanding and many shall have dreams and visions, and many shall see who their Messiah is. Yes, Netanyahu, you are Mine! You are Mine! And I shall move and you shall have night visitations. At first, you shall tell no one. Then you shall tell and share with your son and those around you. Yes, you are Mine! Israel, you are Mine! I'll not let you go. You're the Apple of My Eye. Zechariah 2:8 Yes, there's a time of shaking coming in your land. There's a time of shifting coming in your land. And you're going to shift from the Old Covenant to the New Covenant. That's the better Covenant! Yes, so do you're shifting, do your praying, do your waiting on Me, for soon I AM going to reveal all of who I AM to you. So Israel, there shall be turmoil in the days ahead in your land, but there shall be My blessing; there shall be My provision; there shall be My protection. And I AM going to have you as a people. For, yes, you are the Apple of My Eye and woe unto those who would touch you in the day ahead. Soon I AM going to deal with nations, nations, nations that would like to destroy you. Soon

I AM going to deal with those nations and they will be destroyed. They will be uprooted forever, says the Spirit of the Lord. So rejoice! O Israel! O Israel! My Apple! My Prized Possession!

Mercies Everlasting

July 07, 2013

O taste and see that the Lord is good. Psalms 34:8 For His mercies are new every morning. Lamentations 3:23 His mercies are everlasting. From generation to generation. From the rising of the sun and the setting of the sun and even in the new moon, His mercies are everlasting. Oh, they are glorious and powerful, so taste and see in the days ahead, the beauty of His holiness. For the glory cloud shall move across this great land from one part of this country to another part, but it shall rest over Philadelphia for months and months at a time. And nobody shall hardly be able to move and they will hear about it on the news. They will run to this nation. They shall run to this state. They shall run to this city, Philadelphia, from all around the world. Come one! Come all! Come here, there's healing! They shall truly say. Come one! Come all! They will voice it throughout the nations. The news media shall voice it. They shall truly come here: one by one; two- by-two; groups of many, they shall truly come. From the Far East, the Near East, the Middle East, from Africa, from all parts of the world. Even from Europe. They will come here and they will find My goodness and mercy waiting on them. So prepare your hearts to receive many people. Prepare your minds and souls and bodies to not be weary in well doing for, Me; for yes, you shall reap if you faint not. Galatians 6:9 Think it not strange how I have put you together, for My plan is a wonderful plan for the body of Christ, jointly fit together. I shall have My perfect work as I bring in the Apostles, the Prophets, the Pastors, the Teachers, and the Evangelists. Even as the gifts of the Spirit are in operation, you shall see signs and wonders that you can't even imagine! You shall see the Holy Spirit manifested in such unusual ways. The healings, they shall be dramatic. The miracles shall be wonderful. So give Me the praise. Rejoice even before you see the mighty things, for this age of grace shall soon come to an end, says the Spirit of the Lord.

Philadelphia Lawyers/Philadelphia Evangelists

July 26, 2013

Philadelphia, the Lord says, is known for its lawyers. And there shall be a great move of God among the law firms here in Philadelphia. And they shall be some of the ones that will really spearhead the move of God in Philadelphia, in Center City. They shall lead many prayer groups and shall even be teachers of the Word of God. I shall raise them up in a short time, says the Lord thy God. But more than this, more than the Philadelphia Lawyers and their fame, is the fame that shall spread around the world of the Philadelphia Evangelists.

There shall be many who go out from Philadelphia. There shall be evangelists. Some will be from this area and some I shall bring in and train and raise up to be evangelists. But all of the ones from Philadelphia, they shall go around the world. And this is a time when, as I train them, they will train others. And I will send out the evangelists from Colombia. I will send out the evangelists from London, from the UK, once again. I will even send out evangelists from the Netherlands, from Canada, Australia, and New Zealand and of course, the United States. But the Lord says, I shall send many missionaries from Africa, even into Europe. I shall send many missionaries – and the Philippines shall be a nation of missionaries. I shall raise up many in India to go, and China, and in Korea; especially, to go to the nations.

But the Lord says there shall spread a fame about the anointing of God on the Evangelists from Philadelphia. For I shall have a great move of God. It shall spring up here and it shall go to the nations. And many shall come here from the nations and they shall catch the office of an Evangelist. They shall catch the fervor. They shall catch the passion of My heart. They shall weep before Me. They shall weep for the nations; and, yes, they shall go out to many nations from Philadelphia. Yes, a Name shall be raised up in this city and it shall be My Name, says the Lord thy God. For I shall not share My Fame and My Glory with another. And these ones shall be precious ones, for they shall not desire to have a reputation or a name. But they shall have a desire to publish forth My Name abroad in the days ahead. For great shall be the anointing as they work in signs, wonders, and many miracles, says the Lord thy God. For I shall send them out and it shall be a quick work, and then I will come soon. Yes, many don't believe Me. But yes, I AM coming soon and will not tarry, says the Lord your God.

More Ready Than You Think!

August 07, 2013

The Lord says you're more ready than you think you are.

You're closer to the things you've been praying for than you think you are.

So oh, in the back of your mind, you'd say, the revival, the move of God in Philadelphia is a long ways away. But the Lord says you're closer to the move of God than you think you are. You're closer to hearing the angel blow that trump, that will start the revival in Philadelphia. It's even at hand. For even as the scripture says, not three months and not six months and then the harvest. But the Lord says now is the harvest. It's soon at hand. Soon that angel shall bring with him that great trumpet and blow it over Philadelphia and then everything shall change. But soon there's going to be many suddenlies. Suddenly war. Sudden destruction. Sudden famine. Sudden earthquakes. Many things are getting ready to unfold. For as you get ready to go into 2014, things shall be very different. The weather shall seem to be upside down. Governments shall be upside down. Many governments in the world won't know the right hand from the left hand. The decisions they make shall seem off the wall. But the Lord says, I AM shaking the governments. I AM shaking even the earth. I AM getting ready in the middle of destruction, in the middle of war, to move by My Holy Spirit. I AM going to pour out My Holy Spirit and quench many thirsty lands. Isaiah 44:3 Many countries and many nations are thirsty for Me. Many don't realize it, but when they get a taste of Me, they'll see that I AM the water. Remember the woman in the Bible that I promised her not just a natural water, but a spiritual water? John 4 For the Lord says, yes, the sweet water of the Holy Spirit is getting ready to break forth. Break the vessels. Break the vessels – the pottery of honor that I have stored the holy water in. 2 Timothy 2:20 For the water of My Spirit is getting ready to be poured out on all mankind. Joel 2:20/Acts 2:17 So you are closer than you think. You're more ready than you think. You're closer than you think to seeing your prayers fulfilled. For this ministry. For each and every one in the prayer room's ministry. For you're closer to realizing the answers to your prayers. For the answer is even at hand. It is nigh thee, even in thy mouth. Romans 10:8 So the Lord says just continue to praise Me. You've been pushing. You've been pushing, and you're almost there. The breakthrough is even at hand. So your destiny shall surely come and soon it shall change drastically, says the Lord. So the ones who have been faithful here to pray, I say, yes, your destiny will be fulfilled. The answers to your prayers are on the way, even sooner than you can imagine. Oh, it's closer at hand. So the Lord says, press in there. Push in there. You are more ready than you think. You're closer to getting the answer to your prayers than you realize, says the Spirit of the Lord.

There is A Fire Burning

This prophecy was sung.

October 24, 2013

There's a fire burning.

A refiner's fire.

It is a fullers soap. Cleansing.

The fire will cleanse.

Days of fire.

The fire of the Holy Spirit is burning and cleansing this nation.

I shall clean out New York.

There shall be a move of My Spirit and then that city will go.

The city with the Babylon spirit, New York City, will go.

First a move of God. Pray that many will escape.

And then disaster after disaster will hit New York.

Days of rage, and evil in the streets and people fighting.

Days of rage shall follow as disaster after disaster hits New York.

Watch San Francisco sink.

Watch it sink and become nothing.

Many cities of abomination and on fire.

Burning down.

Fires are raging and burning.

This is the time. It must come to pass.

I'll burn out the abomination of homosexuality.

I'll burn out the abomination of abortion.

Those that have supported it, they shall be burned out.

Fires are burning.

Hear My voice. In the midst of these fires, even in the natural, shall be My Holy Spirit fire burning. In the spiritual, Holy Spirit fires will be burning bright.

You will have need of nothing, for I will take care of you.

Don't worry and don't fear but know what's getting ready to happen.

The die has been cast and there's no turning back.

Days of rage in New York City.

Yet I've got My places of refuge. Philadelphia, you're My refuge. The angels are protecting Philadelphia, My city of Refuge. I have other cities and town of refuge. But there'll be those on fire for their abominations and for their rage against Me. They raged against Me and now look and see at the results of their rage against Me. Burning. Burning. All night long. The fire is unquenchable.

It can't be stopped. They'll burn for days and days. Destruction. New fires burning for days. The fires are bright.

They're unstoppable. But so is My Holy Spirit as He sweeps. The authorities and the evil one cannot stop the move of My Holy Spirit. They shall try but they shall not stop it. They shall try to stop it. Even as the men of Sodom and Gomorrah when they were struck blind, they were pushing at the door. Feeling at the door and trying to get in the door to those angels. Even as the evil men and women are going down and cities are on fire, they'll still be doing evil. They won't repent. They'll be drinking and partying to the very end. Even as they did at the end of WWII in Germany. Even as the end was coming in Berlin, the people did party and drink. Even though they were facing death, they did party and drink. So shall it be in the cities in this land. Cities that are burning but yet they party on. Cities in destruction, but yet they party on. Nothing shall stop them. They are a perverse generation. Be not like them but be My remnant people. Be drawn unto Me.

Come into My arms in this time and season. Rest you will find. Rest you will find. Rest you will find. Rest you will find.

Rest not like earthly rest. But rest from above. Rest from the Holy Spirit. The Holy Spirit's rest you will walk in. In these last days, the Holy Spirit's rest you will surely walk in. Walk in My ways. Walk in the Spirit and you will not fulfill the lust of the flesh. Walk in the Spirit, and you will not be consumed. Walk in the Spirit I say unto you. Walk into the things of the Spirit. Know My Voice.

CHAPTER 4
PROPHECY GOVERNMENTS, MEDIA, FINANCES, SPORT, COMMERCE, ETC.

Destiny of A People

January 24, 2011

Give a shout to the Lord

The whole earth shall be filled with his glory!

From Africa came many tribes and tongues to fulfill a destiny I had called them to fulfill. They came here out of much turmoil, distress and pain. All the people in the earth in this new day shall have their place and shall fulfill what I have called them to do.

The Lord says there shall become a great crisis in the land and the Congress shall be on their knees. It shall be the black race from Africa that shall help save this country. The whites won the freedom for this country, but the blacks shall keep it. There have been laws passed to give equal rights, but still they have not been fully received in society. Out of this crisis shall come a special place of honor in this Nation. Where there have been statues and memorials for whites who served this country, you will now see the same for blacks. Blacks on a whole have shown more zeal for me and they will fulfill my plan in this hour. They will be a vanguard and shall take my message to the world. Also the Latinos, Asians and other groups shall fulfill their call. In this time shall my desire for the nations be fulfilled.

Given to me. January 12, 2011

Shortage. Shortage, Shortage

January 13, 2011

There shall be shortage of oil, food, and clothing. It shall be found that the main problem shall be a distribution problem!

Fall of False Gods

November 04, 2011

For days I have heard God say He is going to deal with the false gods of our society. Listed are the ones and the order He gave me.

1. SPORTS – Psalm 16:4 I had a vision of the gladiators killing Christians and then I saw men in a trance-like state all weekend in front of the TV. Corruption and abuse will be exposed.

2. SHOPPING – For more stuff, excessive buying and hoarding – many malls and shopping centers closed.

3. RELIGION – Preaching a different gospel. Many big name ministries closed – deal with Islam.

4. EDUCATION – a move of God in schools that cannot

be stopped – professors and elite changed!

5. COMMERCE – Stock markets, banks, greed, dishonest business practices will be exposed.

6. GOVERNMENTS – The big lie – Both political parties one in the same. Exposed – Elite who give orders to the President, etc.

7. MEDIA – Lies, distortions unfolded, movies, TV.

8. GOD OF SELF – "I DID IT MY WAY!"

Raising up A People

January 20, 2012

I'll raise up a people young and old, small and great, children, oh, they shall go to the nations. The captive shall be set free. Yes, a mighty separation is coming in My body in this country. Oh, I'm going to separate those false brethren from you in this country. I'm going to raise up My true church. Oh yes I'm finished with the religious in this country. I'm raising up My church. I shall not tolerate insurrection in the body of Christ anymore. I shall not tolerate ministries based on "me, me, me." Oh I must have ministries based on ME. On Me. On Me and My Word. Only My Word and I through the Holy Spirit shall set the captive free!

Only I and My Word shall be able to set the captive free. For there are many in bondage in this country. Oh, many, many, many, many shall be set free and the demons shall cry and come out of them, says the Lord. There's great deliverance coming to this country. Oh, but it will not be easy for they are resisting Me. For they are resisting Me. But I've heard your cry. I've heard you remind me of the covenant that I made with William Penn and others like William Penn in this country. I made a covenant. I shall keep My covenant but it's going to be rough. There's going to be turmoil. There's going to be up and downs. Oh, but I shall reach this people. They've turned into a stubborn people, just like Israel. But I know how to reach them. I know how to get to this nation. Oh, I'm dealing with this nation right now. I'm dealing with this nation and their thoughts and their purposes in this election. It won't be easy. This is not an easy time for the government. It's not an easy time for the Congress. It's not an easy time for the stock market. For the financial institutions. I'm going to shake them all till they're down on their knees before Me.

It's a great year. This is a great year. This is a great year for My glory to come in this country. In the midst of turmoil and upset – oh, yes, the apple cart's upset. Yes I'm going to right the apple cart. But the apples are going to be rolling everywhere. Oh, many in the natural shall try to gather the apple back and put them in the cart – but it won't be possible. It won't be possible. The only thing that will be possible is for those to come into My kingdom. When those come into My Kingdom. I shall right the apple cart. When those come into My Kingdom in sufficient numbers, Yes, I shall move in this great land. I haven't forgot about your prayers. I haven't forgot about the prayers of others. I'll keep My covenant, but I'm going to deal – I'm going to deal with those who have tried to destroy this land. I'm going to deal with them. You shall see many important people in Hollywood in the news media, in the government – you will see them drop dead in the days to come. And many false ministers you will see them drop dead in the days ahead. They're going to be eaten up and consumed by disease. They're going to have accidents. They're going to drop by the wayside. Some of them will even go insane.

But the Lord says. Be steady! Oh, be steady before Me. Don't be moved by what you see or hear. Don't you worry or be in fear. Oh, don't fret or be in fear for I've got the whole situation under control. Days of terror. Days of torment. Days of great distress in this country are coming. But don't you fear, I will protect you. I will protect you from the evil one. Never, never take thought for tomorrow for your every need shall be supplied. Even in that which is to come.

The shortages, even the famine, even that which is to come – I will take care of you. I will take care of you in the turmoil. Fret not because of he who prospers in his way. For I shall not tolerate those that would come against My remnant people in this time. I will not tolerate them. I will not tolerate those who come against Israel in this time. This is a different time. This is a different season. Watch and pray. Watch and pray. And see what I will do, says the Lord of Hosts.

Broken Walls

March 08, 2012

This country is like Jerusalem, as in the days of Nehemiah where the walls were broken down. Oh, yes, even the walls in this country in the natural are broken down. So anybody can leave or come as they please into this country or go out, without any restraints.

Yes, the walls are broken down. Yes, they're broken down by Planned Parenthood, ACLU, by the news Medias, by Hollywood. The walls are broken down by the religious. The walls are broken down by enemies from abroad. The walls are broken down so that people are in fear. Oh, yes even the banks – even the financial institutions have caused usury in this country, even as there was in Jerusalem. For the people in famine because of the usury. The banks and the financial people at that time. Even as this is a type of Jerusalem in Nehemiah's time – yes, the Sanballat's that are on the wall laughing and mocking – but the Lord says, watch Me. One by one, I'll shut them down. Watch Me.

The Sanballat's that would come against Me and Nehemiah spirits in this hour, I will bring them down. Yes, I'm raising up a people that have a Nehemiah spirit or that who have the spirit of Ezra. Yes, I shall use those men and women to shut down every spirit of opposition. Every spirit that has tried to destroy what this country is about. Oh, yes, I shall shut them down, even as I did him. For you have the backing of a

King that is greater the Prince of Persia. You have My backing. And I AM the Lord, the Mighty God and I will protect you. I will have My way in this country. And I will use you even as you watch and pray to rebuild the walls of this country: politically, economically, but most of all spiritually. You shall rebuild the walls of this country and it shall be strong once again, says the Lord.

Exposed!

November 08, 2012

There shall be much pain and unrest in this great land as I expose those who strive to rule the world and operate in the background to bring about global government. There shall be a great shaking in the capitals of many nations as these people are smoked out of their secret hiding places by the Holy Spirit. They think they are hidden from public view and can plot their evils. I will expose them (the Illuminati) just as I did several hundred years ago in France, Austria, and Germany, as they tried to bring rebellion and revolution to those nations. This is a day when I will expose, expose, expose! They are the quiet powers behind communism and Islam. They finance these movements and think they will never be caught when they fail. I will expose them and their puppets in several nations. There shall be great tumult and uproar!

Nations and governments will be overthrown by Me. They will be like rats that flee a sinking ship, like roaches running from light to darkness as they are exposed by the Holy Spirit. It shall be a dangerous time such as the world has never seen, and worldwide financial collapse will shock all! Men shall weep and howl! Things will never be the same in this global economy as fear and dread are everywhere! There shall be a shocking move of God that shall not be stopped in all the world, and then I will come! You see, these men will have to be uprooted so the anti-christ can come to the forefront. There is no honor among thieves. And these people will turn on each other as they are betrayed by Lucifer! Satan will laugh and mock at them as they fall, for they believed they were god-like and a power unto themselves. As Satan supported and made them filthy rich, he will now pull the rug out from under their feet. Yes, there is a great sifting and shaking in the nations. I laugh at mere men and their foolish ways, for who is like unto Me? They shall be exposed where most of them reside – in Switzerland. There is a great move of God coming to that small nation and there shall be a bright light shining forth out of Bern.

I shall move the resources out of the banking centers in Switzerland into My remnant people's hands. Many leaders in governments will be imprisoned as they are exposed. The great light of My Holy Spirit move that shall start in Bern will spread and will shine on their evil deeds. Yes, I will do a quick work in the nations and then I will come quickly!

Be faithful, My saints, My dear ones, My overcomers, for the day of revealing the evil one is almost here. Yes, soon shall be the Great Day of the Lord!

*Psalms Chapter 2

*James 5: 1-6

*Revelations 18

*Revelations 16:19

Time, Time, Time

November 25, 2012

One time will soon end and a new time will be.

Time is changing!

Gentile time is coming to an end.

In a short while we will be back on Jewish times. So, My Elect, know the times and seasons. Know My Doctrines, My Holy Word and walk in it.

The time has come when many people's doctrines will not be sound. Walk with Me, and examine your life according to My Word. From now on, events will seem to happen almost overnight. Events in Israel will change the earth, especially My Church. Israel and the Body of Christ will become more closely linked in thought and actions. Soon Israel's eyes will be more fully opened to who I AM. My many events in Israel will spark a great move of God in all the nations. In this move, you will start to see who are the sheep and goat nations that I will separate in the future. These goat nation s will take harsh actions against Christians and Jews, but it will bring them together to support each other. Israel will be a great military power and evil nations will be afraid.

Israel will have new technologies, techniques, and procedures so sophisticated that it will cause current weapons to become obsolete. The military powers and products will be turned upside down and a new order will develop in military science.

Fear not, for the shaking must happen because I come! Look for Me! The days are shortened. Behold I come quickly and will not tarry.

Pope Removed – Elite Exposed

February 12, 2013

They removed the Pope, who I had allowed them to set in place, for they are an evil, impatient generation, more evil than their fathers. Their great lust for evil shall be their downfall as they are exposed before the world, while they live in luxury in the secret high places of Switzerland, Luxembourg, and Lichtenstein. The anti-christ spirit, which has enriched, empowered and hidden them for centuries, will be exposed by the Holy Spirit.

They will be revealed for who and what they are. Their power will be broken before the evil one, the anti-christ, comes, for he will share his power with no one. Satan has now broken his pact with them and will laugh in derision as they fall, losing their status and wealth before the elite of the world systems. Few people even among the elite know who they really are and how they direct and influence many systems. First and foremost, I will deal with the religions of the world, one by one. Now, I am starting with the false religions from Rome, then Islam, which I will use Israel to destroy. Then, one by one, I will make the other false gods as dung. Next, I will upset financial, education, military, political and government systems of the world.

The elites have lived where their power centers of finance were. Every other system of man rotates around the love of money. "Where your treasure is, is where your heart shall also be." Matthew 6:21. The kingdoms of this present world shall come to naught, for didn't I say in My Scriptures, that "I change the times and the seasons, remove kings, set up kings, and give wisdom to the wise and knowledge to them that know and understand? I reveal the deep secret things and those ones will know what is in the darkness and my light dwells within them!" Daniel 2:21-22. Soon, I will remove them from the mountain tops even as they have removed the Pope.

Who are those ones who I reveal My secret plans to at this time? My special remnant people who stay before Me in prayer and devotion, praising Me in their coming and going, a vast vanguard company who will go forth to every nation with My Word. I will anoint them and empower them with signs and wonders by the Holy Spirit. They shall have the wealth that is talked about in Proverbs that the wicked heap and store in secret places. I had them store it up not for them, but for

My people, for this great end time move of God. A last great end time move of God has started and it shall go around the world. Philadelphia will be on everyone's lips as pockets of revival spring up out of that "City of Brotherly Love."

The days are shortened. Time is running out! If I didn't shorten the time, all flesh would be destroyed by the evil one by disease, famine, and war. Great upheaval is now coming in every part of the world. Chaos and confusion like the world has never seen. I will bring forth My people in this time of confusion and they will shine like the brightest stars as they share My Son, Jesus Christ, with all the world.

Be not in fear, as the "Time of the Gentiles" comes to an end. This is the time spoken of and all these things must come to an end. So, "study to show yourselves approved, a workman that will not be put to shame, rightly dividing the word of truth." 2 Timothy 2:15. Know My Word, My doctrines. Preach about My power to save, heal, deliver and set the captives free and give recovering of sight to the blind. "Be instant in season and out of season. Reprove, rebuke, exhort and teach even the little ones to know and hear My voice. 2 Timothy 4:2. Prepare the way for the soon coming of your Lord and Savior, Jesus Christ!

As soon as God spoke to me about the Pope, the Holy Spirit asked me these questions. We can ask God what He would be willing to show us and ponder.

1. Why do the Pope and Vatican have Swiss security guards whom they pay? Why not have German or Italian,

etc.? Who pays them and for what purposes? It seems to me that their purposes would be to protect not so much the Pope, but the total interests of the elite who live in Switzerland, etc., who try to control the world and guard their special positions.

2. Why didn't Hitler invade Switzerland, Luxembourg and Lichtenstein – German speaking countries? He said he wanted to unite all Germanic people under one umbrella. That was his excuse as several countries were invaded. I believe Hitler and his cronies wanted to hide their wealth stolen from Jews and other countries. Also he was afraid to disturb the elite bankers, etc. who financed him and Germany's war machine. They had power over him because the fallen spirits that control them were of a higher order than the ones controlling Hitler. Satan ranks his army, just as God has ranks among His angels.

The Lord showed to me that the amount of loot the Nazi's stole from the Jewish people has never really been exposed. Only a small amount some years ago. It will be, and some of this money will go into Israel and much of it will find its ways into end time Jewish people who will preach Jesus Christ in the end times.

*The Prophecy Exposed, 11/18/12 connects to this information.

Unraveled – Revealed

February 14, 2013

It started in 2008 and has continued to happen more and more every year. Things have started to unravel and there is not an individual, a nation, a government, or financial institution that can or shall be able to stop what I AM doing. Things shall continue to unravel, and there shall be an unveiling and revealing of corruption, intrigue, terror, deceit, yes, all manner of deception, and I shall remove the covers and let all the world see things naked before Me that can no longer be hidden.

Just as Adam and Eve knew they were now naked before Me, the nations shall be uncovered before Me and man. Religions, financial groups, governments, schools, etc., shall all be seen by mankind as they really are. There shall be a shaking that will have a chilling effect on everyone and commerce shall be turned upside down.

There shall be utter chaos and confusion for days in financial markets and governments for days at a time. It shall be like a roller coaster ride with all the highs and lows of the "she said," "he said," "they did." The world shall seem to be totally undone: Suicides of many in important positions, and surely there shall be distress of nations. The time is short, and as I uncover the corruption and the anti-christ spirit in the world that totally is against My Body of Believers, Israel and Me, I will reveal Who I really AM in all My power and glory. My glory and power will be so strong in the earth that no one speaking in truth will be able to deny Who I AM for they will know in their hearts that there is a living God and that there is, without a doubt, only one way and that is by the blood of His Son, Jesus Christ!

Yes, I will be in the temple, the market place, not with a whip, but I AM coming with a sword to undo all that man and satan have done. I will start to bring My order into the nations, for I AM the Holy One of Israel, Lord of Lords, King of Kings, and the Soon Coming Savior of the World.

So rejoice and don't be in fear for all this must happen before I come: distress of nations, war, famine and destruction. Matt 10:34, Hebrews 4.

Prayer Burden

February 14, 2013

Dying and going to hell.

Dying and going to hell.

Dying and going to hell.

So many people are getting ready to die.

Oh, so many people are getting ready to die.

Oh God! Help me!

Oh God! Help me!

Help me to make it through, Lord God.

Help me to make it through, Lord God.

Tongues.

Groaning.

Oh, Lord, give me rest and peace.

Oh, Lord God!

Oh, Lord God!

Something's getting ready to happen.

Something terrible.

Something – Oh, Lord God!

Be with all these people.

Be with all these people.

Be with the nations.

The nations. Be with the nations.

Oh, Lord God! Is it the big war in the Middle East? Is that the destruction that's coming, Lord God? Oh, millions dying. Millions dying. Millions dying. Is this it, Lord? Millions upon millions dying, Lord God. Is this it? Oh, Lord God – what is it? Let this thing pass. Let this burden pass off of me, Lord God.

Tongues.

Weighed. Weighed. Weighed in the balances and found wanting. Even as Belshazzar was weighed in the balances and was found wanting. Daniel 5:27.

Oh, Lord God, there's nations, there's nations, there's nations – there's nations weighed in the balances and found wanting. Nations. Nations. Nations. In the balances and found wanting. Nations. Nations. Nations.

It's night. I can see God's handwriting on the wall. As they were in their party, as they were drinking wine and strong drink out of the vessels of the Temple of God, - God said, 'No more! No more! No more! No more!'

Weighed in balances and found wanting. Nations. Nations. Destruction is coming. Destruction is coming. Destruction is coming. People shall holler 'Peace and Safety.' Soon you will see people hollering, 'Peace and Safety' in this country and in the nations of the world, but there is coming sudden destruction. 1 Thessalonians 5:3. There is coming sudden destruction such as the world has never seen. Nations and whole groups of people weighed in the balances and found wanting. They're found wanting. They've come against God. They've come against the Apple of His Eye, Israel. They've come against the Body of Christ.

God is going to deal with those who've come against Israel. God is going to deal – I don't know if it's a war coming – if it's the Psalms 83 war coming soon – but there is destruction coming. War and destruction. War and destruction. War and destruction such as the world has never known. Millions and millions of people involved in this war. Millions and millions of people.

All of this must come to pass. All of this must come to pass.

The burden is so great. The burden - Oh, the burden. I feel it deep in my spirit. I feel it in the pit of my stomach. A sick feeling. A sick feeling. A feeling of despair in the pit of my stomach for all these people. A burden and despair for all of these people who are going to die.

Tongues. But it must be. It must be. This is the time. This is the season that was spoken of by the prophets of old. All prophecy – all things must be fulfilled. This is that season. This is that time we're going into. A different season. A different chapter in the history of the earth. The ending of one chapter and the beginning of another. The end of this chapter will not be a happy ending for many nations and many people. I'm going to show My glory and power in all the earth. I'm going to show My power. I'm going to show My power and then I'll show My glory. There shall be a turning to Me, after this, all around the earth. There shall be no denying who I AM. I AM He who sits above the circle of the earth and men look as mere grasshoppers to Me. Isaiah 40:22.

Nations seem as dung before Me. Oh, yes. I said, 'Touch not My prophets nor do My people any harm.' You have done harm to My people and now you'll be repaid. You will be repaid for your sins have come upon you. For your sins are coming upon you! Nations! Hear the voice of God! Your sins are coming upon you. Nations shall never be the same. Forever changed. Things shall be changed forever, even before I come.

Tongues.

After this destruction there will be a great turning unto Me. Many nations and people turning unto Me. Some turning to Me for the first time. Some returning unto Me. Many nations that once knew Me returning unto Me. Nations that have never really known Me coming unto Me.

Yes, after this destruction shall begin a great move of God that shall sweep whole nations in to the Kingdom of God. Whole nations shall be swept into the Kingdom of God. Oh, but first this destruction must come. First this distress must come. First this upheaval must come. And then a great turning unto Me.

They'll be seeking out the believers. Those around you will be seeking out the believers. Truly, they'll be coming to Philadelphia. Every tribe. Every tongue. Every language. Every kind of people coming unto Philadelphia. They're coming to Philadelphia. Coming. Coming. Coming. Prepare ye the way of the Lord.

Offer yourself as a sacrifice unto the Lord. Oh, yes, even as the Lord came to Samuel – and Eli said, 'When He comes again, say, yes! Lord! I'm here. Speak, Lord!' So, we're going to be saying, 'Speak to us, Lord!' Yes! Lord! Speak to us! We'll hear Your voice. We'll do Your bidding. We'll go where You want us to go. We'll go to the nations. We'll go to every tribe and tongue.

We'll go forth in great joy with the victory. Out of Philadelphia, many shall go to the nations. First, the nations shall come to Philadelphia and then many out of Philadelphia shall go back to the nations – shall go to many nations. Oh, you can't imagine how it will be. You can't imagine the spark that will start the fire in Philadelphia. Oh, it will surprise you. It won't start where you would expect it to start but it will surprise you how I will do it. How I will do it.

I will get the glory, not man. I'll not share My glory with another. For I'm coming soon. Prepare ye the way. I'm not coming back riding on a donkey. I'm not coming back riding on a burro that's borrowed. But I'm coming back riding on a white horse. I'm King of Kings and Lord of Lords. Oh, yes, in all My glory. With angels surrounding Me. With the saints around Me. Oh, yes. Caught up in His glory.

Be caught up in His glory today. Be caught up in the glory cloud today. Let Him find you actively seeking His face. Those who are actively seeking My face, My glory and My power will come on those. Those that have been waiting as it were in the upper room. My glory and power will come on those ones. Those who have been waiting before Me. Those of insignificance. Those who have been waiting in the small rooms all around the world - where the remnant has gathered. Those are the ones I'm coming to. Those are the ones I'm going to visit. Those are the ones I'm going to be with. Those are the ones I'm going to share My power with. And they'll walk in My glory. I'll share My secrets with these ones. These precious ones. Oh, yes, they'll be the vanguard company. They'll be the vanguard company that will go out in great power and lead this move of God.

A great move of God it is surely.

A great move of God it is surely.

It is something surely to behold. Governments shall tremble. Financial institutions shall tremble. Commerce shall tremble. Everyone shall tremble at My power and glory.

They shall tremble when My saints come into their presence. They shall tremble and fall on their knees when My saints come into their presence, and they'll say, 'What must I do to be saved?' They will weep and howl and repent before Me. Kings, Rulers, Presidents, yes, they'll be down on their knees. Nations will be down on their knees. Before the Day of the Lord, nations shall be down on their knees before Me. Whole nations. Whole nations shall be down on their knees before that great day of the Lord. For surely that great day of the Lord is coming soon.

You've entered into that time. It's close to that time. So watch and wait. Watch and wait and stay before Me. Keep your lamps trimmed. For you know not the time or the hour when I will come. Trim your lamps . Trim the lights. Keep the fuel full in the lamps, for I AM coming.

I AM coming.

I AM coming in all My glory. Oh, My children, wait for Me. Wait for Me. Wait for Me.

"My Little Ones" U.S.A

February 28, 2013

Children, children, this is a time when I will really reach out to the children and youth. I shall move upon them in homes, but most of all I shall really move in the schools. I shall really move in the great universities and go all the way down to kindergartens. As the scripture says, a child shall lead them. I shall really move among the children, youth, and college students in the days ahead. The school officials shall be dumbstruck as I move like a fire throughout the school systems. I will bring the Bible back to the classrooms, prayer back to their assembly programs. Yes, they shall try to stop it each and every way, but I shall stop them. They will try to get the courts to stop it, but every time the judges open their mouths, they shall look foolish and shall not even be able to complete their sentences. I shall then move from the schools to the courthouses to the courtrooms for days at a time. It shall seem to be chaos and confusion, but then you will see a pattern where the judges and their spectators shall be on their knees before Me. It shall be as a hush, and a holy awe as they weep before Me and as I move in all My power and glory. They shall weep and cry out as they ask Me for forgiveness for the wrong judgments they made. They shall cry out to God for salvation until everyone in the rooms shall be down on their knees before Me. They shall weep and howl and cry out unto Me for all the murders of unborn babies. It shall be quite an affair to take in!

Then Congress shall become involved and try to stop this great move of God, but I shall stop them and have them down on their knees. I shall reveal those who have an anti-christ spirit and who are communist and they shall be put to shame and openly scorned as the truth comes out. It shall really shake the nations for days and days. For I will reveal who I AM for I will no longer tolerate what they have done to My children. It would be better if they had a millstone tied around their necks than to do the evil they have done for years to My precious little ones. Their blood cries out to Me from all the earth and I shall deal with the evil ones in My own way and I shall stop them in their evil ways. I will expose, expose the great evil in the government and every institution and organization will be shaken in this time. I will expose Wall Street, financial markets, and all the banking systems. This is just the beginning, for I will shake the kingdoms of the earth in these last days. I will move by My Holy Spirit and nothing shall be able to stop Me! Things have shifted in the earth. It is a different time and a new season which I AM now starting, My saints. I have heard your prayers for years and now I AM moving! The time is short, so get ready for all to be fulfilled for I AM coming soon and will not delay!

Mysterious Events

March 07, 2013

Things are going to fit together like pieces of a puzzle.

A mystery. A mystery. Mysterious days. Mysterious events.

Things that are hidden in the dark are coming out. All the pieces of the puzzle are fitting together in the days ahead. Oh, yes! The plans that I have for the nations will be revealed in the days ahead. You'll see the plans that I have for different nations: For this country, for Russia, for China, Oh, for other countries. For Israel, Jordan, Turkey, the Sudan. You'll see the plans that I have for these countries in the days ahead. It will be very evident in the days ahead the sheep nations and the goat nations. It will be very evident ahead, who's for Me and who's against Me. It will be interesting. It will be thought provoking and really strange in the days ahead. Nations that were enemies will now become friends. Nations that were friends will now become enemies.

An uproar. A turmoil. You shall see things fit together. You'll wonder in amazement and then you'll realize, "Oh, yes! We saw a picture of this a little while back! We saw this coming but we didn't completely understand." The Lord says things are going to be clearer – even in the short period ahead. Things are going to be much clearer about how I'm going to move in the end times; about what My plans are; about how the kingdoms are rising, and what kingdoms are going down. It's going to be very evident, without question, and you will really know what's happening.

To you, My remnant people, I'm going to speak, and you'll understand the new time and the new season that we're walking in. For it shall be different in the world, very shortly, than it ever has in the history of mankind. But also, what's old shall become new again, and what's new shall become old news. So you shall see time and time again such a shifting that you can't even imagine. It shall shock all the financial markets. It shall shock the governments. It shall shock traditional alliances. For things shall not remain the same. But even as the end time days come right before you, you shall be caught up in it yourself, for you shall be in the end time move of God. And yet I shall shake the nations; I shall destroy kingdoms with My Word, for My Word shall prevail. For I, the Lord Jesus Christ, shall prevail in this time! And even the nations as they rage against Me in the days ahead, I shall ignore them, for their time is short. For in the midst of confusion, in the midst of decay, in the midst of turmoil, in the midst of earthquakes, which will happen more frequently, and larger and larger in the day ahead……..Oh, yes, as you see strange signs in the heavens, even know that surely the coming of the Lord is soon! And I will not stay away from My Bride much longer, says the Lord thy God. I'm coming for a people; I'm coming for a bride. So the Lord says have discernment. Know the times and the seasons. Look for Me. Keep your lamps full of oil and trimmed, for I shall come soon. Be not caught unawares of the times and the seasons and when I'm coming, for I shall do a quick work. You'll be surprised how quick the work will be. And then I'll come for My people, My saints, MY remnant, precious ones, says the Spirit of Grace.

Checkmate

March 08, 2013

In the days ahead, the earth shall seem like a chess board with all the players making their moves. Russia loves chess and I shall move Russia around on My chess board in the days ahead. Russia shall think they are powerful and are making their moves, but I laugh, for I AM whispering in their ear to move here and there. Russia is involved in many end time events. The alliances that Russia and other nations develop in the end times shall be strange, but you shall see My hand and purpose and know it is of Me. So don't be concerned with Russia and China, for I have My special plans for them and soon you shall start to see things develop. Yes, there shall always be a Russia, but in the time period ahead, you will be amazed what shall happen there!

War and more conflicts, disasters, days of confusion and days of not having complete understanding of several worldwide situations shall soon be. Leaders and nations shall be caught off guard. They shall be surprised and amazed! In a strange and round-about way, I shall use Russia to protect the USA in the days ahead, when her (USA) military is, for a season, weakened and uncertain.

In this game of chess, I shall use Russia to checkmate China. With her new wealth and power, China is emboldened and ascending before the time I have set for her on the world stage. In many ways, China is like a big bully; however, she will be found to be a paper tiger! Russia's military shall checkmate her in the days ahead. Russia and China both fear the USA, and are happy to see her decline, but Russia doesn't want the USA to decline too much, because she worries about China and their population. The Chinese are slowing moving into Russia and this has caused alarm bells to go off, especially with their population in decline. Russia will make a secret agreement with the USA to contain China and this will scare and provoke China when their spy agency uncovers this plot. The USA shall provide much military intelligence to Russia, along with computer attacks against China. It shall be interesting, but at the same time, strange how things are changing

The USA and Russia shall work together on secret projects in the Ural Mountains. Vietnam shall work with the USA and Russia against China. China will have much to fear as Japan and the USA work against her in the Pacific Regions, while Russia in the East and North makes her great pincher moves, Vietnam will move in the South. India shall assert, herself, in the situation also. There shall even be a threat of nuclear war, but Russia shall frustrate and shall make China's escape impossible and China shall suffer defeat and suffer great financial losses. As a result of all this tension, there shall be a shaking in commerce and the financial markets. Great fear shall develop and in this shaking, nations shall be turned upside down for many months to come. Some will never fully recover. In all this period of time, many shall die and there shall be famine and shortages of goods in many nations. This is the end of the end time days and the world will rock and reel at the tension caused by instant daily news. While war clouds are moving, oceans shall be roaring and in this, an increase in earthquakes. Days of fear and worry, but, My Precious ones, don't concern yourselves with situations, but consider Me, Who knows the beginning from the end, and all your goings and comings! I will rise and destroy all My enemies. The time is short, so look for Me. I AM coming soon!

Future Events in Nations

March 08, 2013

Nations are in the balances and found wanting. Nations upon nations upon nations in the wrong place and on the wrong side of God. God is going to start dealing with the nations. He's going to start dealing with the nations, even as He is dealing with Israel right now even as He is dealing with Israel's leadership. He's testing their motives and is seeing where they are. He's calling Israel unto Himself. He's calling Netanyahu unto Himself. Netanyahu's going to start having night visions. He's going to have a revelation of Who I AM, says the Lord. Netanyahu and his son and many others in the government are going to have divine strategies from Me. They'll have a visitation. They're going to even see Me, as I appear unto them in the days ahead. All the many nations which are coming against Israel shall be judged. The time is short. The time is short. The time is short. Nations are soon to be judged. The sheep from the goat nations is becoming more evident all the time.

Look and see and discern and know the times and the seasons that are on us. Yes! Sudden destruction is coming. There shall be sudden destruction over here and over there.

And you shall hear rumors of wars and great evils in the earth. At the same time, wars are happening and wars in process; at the same time shall be earthquakes, and floods and tsunamis. Everything shall be one after another. People will not be able to catch their breath before the other news comes and catches them into the next event. People's hearts shall fear them. Yes, it shall truly be a turning to me in many nations. Nations that have known Me shall start to turn back to Me. as they realize what's happening. Other nations that never knew Me, they'll turn to Me in this time.

I weep because My body of believers, as a whole, is not prepared. They're not prepared. They'll be swept away. Many will be swept away. So I charge you, My Remnant People, you know who you are – know Me. Know My ways. Let your vision for the end time days be expanded, for I have given My Remnant People, each and every one of you, a vision of what you are to do in the end times. Prepare ye the way, for the Lord is coming soon! Prepare yourselves to do the vision that I have placed in your heart. Each has a part to play. The Body of Christ must come together - jointly fit together. All the fiber? All the ligaments need to be fit together. Know your place on the wall. Take your stand. Be not deterred. Be not pushed back by the enemy. Be not pushed back by schools or governments or even military. Be not pushed back from the thing I've called you to do, for I shall give you the power. I shall give you the boldness and nothing shall be able to touch you – even a hair on your head. I'll protect you in the days ahead. Fear not the authorities, as they come against you, but speak boldly for Me, for I shall cause many to come before authorities. I shall cause them to testify of Me and witness for Me and speak boldly the way that they should go, boldly the way their nation should go in the days ahead. For I have a people everywhere in every nation across the whole face of the earth. My people, who have been hidden in secret, are going to rise up at this time.

Smoke and Mirrors

March 15, 2013 "Ides of March"

The Holy Spirit is speaking to me and saying from this day forward there shall be substantial change in how things are done, and there shall begin much change in the world. Things shall begin to change slowly at first and then speed up. Almost every day there will seem to be a great event of some sort of emergency somewhere in the earth. A new reality will soon set in and there shall be much dread and fear. This is a time I will empower My remnant people with a yoke breaking anointing, and they will truly minister in great power and boldness and set the captive free. People at large will feel their love, but also many will walk in fear, dread, and even awe at the miracles, signs, and healings that take place at their hands. My people will have no fear and great boldness so that men of renown shall take note of them and desire to be in their presence. Many shall have the wrong motives and want only to learn their ways so they profit from them. They will all be exposed! This shall surely be a season of smoke and mirrors as I expose, expose the deceit, falsehood, betrayal, and outlandish lies in religion, business, financial markets, governments, politics, sports, etc. I AM starting with all the smoke and mirrors of the Vatican. There is an evil stench in My nostrils as they talk about black and white smoke. All the incense, candles, holy water, bells, icons, etc. The masses they perform are a sham and falsehood and I will expose it. It was meant to keep the people in fear and ignorant of My ways and plans for their lives. I will bring down that woman, that whore, that false prophet, yes, that false system will be destroyed and Rome in ruins. I will expose mega evangelical churches, especially mega churches that operate like Rome with their falsehoods, false doctrine, love of money, and the way they raise funds for their own gain when they are supposed to be for My work. Where in My Word did I instruct them to build huge buildings and an empire for themselves? All smoke and mirrors!

Next, the smoke and mirrors of government, political parties, kingdoms, financial markets will be totally exposed. The masons and secret societies will finally be revealed for all the world to see with all their ugliness. Those who live in the high places in Europe and control the governments and financial markets will be totally undone. Yes, they will turn on each other. More and more governments will fall and impact all financial markets. I will reveal how they all work together to squeeze the people of many nations. In these end time days, My children, don't worry or be in fear as you see the collapse of nations. Put your trust in Me and I will provide your every need as the foundations of society fall apart all around you. Just rest in My promises.

Oh, yes! Give the burdens unto Me. Give the prayer burdens unto Me, for only I can bear them. So rest. Relax. Be peaceful. Be steadfast. Be before Me. Let My burdens and My yoke not be hard on you, but let My burdens and My yoke be easy. For I have made a way for you through the wilderness. I have made a way for you through the famine days which are coming. I have made a way for you through the drought. I have made a way for you through the days of shortage. I have made a way for you through the warfare, in the spiritual and the natural that is surely coming. I AM making a way for My people in the days ahead, even as I made a way out of Egypt. Even as I prepared a place before David in the midst of his enemies, I shall prepare a way for My remnant people, even in the midst of their enemies. I shall raise you up to be a strong voice in many nations. They shall be confounded and confused as you stand. They shall fear your face and be in dread as they see you. They shall fall down on their knees in conviction before you, because in you they shall see a holy God walking upon the earth.

So walk on the earth as giants! Walk upon the earth as spiritual giants in the days ahead, for you are mighty. In Me, you are mighty conquerors. So go forth and conquer. This is the time to conquer. This is not the time to turn back into perdition. This is not the time to shy away, but this is the time to be bold for Me. And you'll see My Holy Spirit boldness in your lives more and more even in the days ahead. So don't despair. Don't think that you can't come up to the task. For I have prepared you for the task, for the job. So find what your hand can do, for I have called each and every one to a purpose. Find what My will is for you and fulfill your destiny. For your destiny is yet before you. Great days of destiny! Oh and I shall use this nation once again. So don't be in fear, for I shall use this nation once again to take the gospel to many, says the Lord your God.

Future Events

March 20, 2013

Events. Events. Events.

The events taking place right now and in the next three months shall shape the destiny of nations. Events taking place right now shall have a great effect on what will happen in the next three years, says the Lord. Oh, yes! Watch the days ahead, for the next three months or so, for you shall surely see decisions made and things done in the earth. Pay careful attention, for you shall see signs that I will give you about what is to take place.

Events. Events. Many events shall take place in the next several months, and you will see things unfold. You'll really see My hand move. And if you have eyes to see, if you have ears to hear and you can see into the things of the Spirit, you will know what is to come. For I will reveal it all around you. I shall reveal it in nature. I shall reveal it in the news. I shall reveal My signs in the heavens. Stop! Look! Listen! Hear what the Spirit of God would expressly say to you in these end time days, in these next several months for decisions made by governments and by peoples. It shall really denote and take them into their destinies.

Nations are in the balances and found wanting. They're making decisions that would cause their destiny to fulfill for the good or for the bad, says the Lord thy God.

Israel - Temple Rebuilt

April 20, 2013

I hear the Lord saying, all scripture must be fulfilled before I come back. Before I come back – and before My feet touch the Mount of Olives, and it is split in half, all scripture must be fulfilled. Scripture must be fulfilled.

I hear the sound of workmen. I hear the sound of saws and stone masons. They're building; they're building the Temple. Oh, yes, the Lord is saying clearly that soon the Temple will be rebuilt on the Temple mound. On the spot that Abraham purchased, it shall be rebuilt. It shall be rebuilt on the Temple mound. It shall be rebuilt.

I hear the sound of preparation. They're busy making

plans. Soon it will be revealed, and quickly shall it be. Oh, it shall go up quickly because the plans have been made. So sing your song of victory; for soon the Temple will be rebuilt and all things will be fulfilled, according as the scripture said.

But before that day that the Temple is rebuilt, it shall be horrible. There will be days of destruction. Days of warfare. It shall be horrible - the destruction that is about to take place in the earth. The Temple will be rebuilt, but first comes war and sudden destruction. Yes, they'll even shout peace, but war is coming. The Lord is saying war is coming. So I'm saying, prepare ye the way of the Lord. Yes, the way of the Lord is being prepared for He is coming soon. But before that, certain events must take place in the earth. So be not weary in well doing. Don't walk in fear but walk in the God kind of faith. Know this: All these things must come to pass before I come. But I will come back in all My glory. I'll come back in a different way than I went, says the Lord. But all these things must be fulfilled, before I come.

Look for the signs all around you. Look at the signs. You can see the great destruction that is coming. You can feel it coming more and more every day, for soon it will visit the earth. It will be a tremendous time on the earth, such as never has been before. But listen! Watch for Me! Look for Me! See My hands moving behind the scenes. I will protect Israel in this time. I will intervene on their behalf. The Lord says, yes, all this must be fulfilled that was spoken of by the prophets. Jer 30.

War, Earthquakes and Famines

April 10, 2013

War, Earthquakes and Famines.

War, Earthquakes and Famines.

Soon you shall see earthquakes and war and destruction, and there will come famine such as you have never seen. Oh, the mighty, mighty earthquakes - several of them - are coming soon, and wars in the future, such as you have never seen. Oh there shall be such a shaking of governments, there shall be such a shaking of economies and political systems. And when you see all this, you will know that soon, there will be a mighty move of God. Following all this, there will be a mighty move of God that will also shake the earth, and then I will come. Then I will come. Then I will come, says the Lord. But look for these times. Know the signs and the seasons and you'll be prepared, and you'll know when they're ready to come to Philadelphia. First there must come all of these horrible things, but then the blessings of the Precious Holy Spirit shall come unto the lives of many people and the captives will be set free, says the Lord.

Humpty Dumpty

April 16, 2013

As the story goes, I hear the Lord reminding me that Humpty Dumpty had a great fall. All the kings' horses and all the kings' men couldn't put Humpty Dumpty back together again. Many governments are going to fall. Many people in governments are going to be exposed and fall. Many countries are going to be exposed and fall. Many economic systems are going to be exposed and fall. They'll try to put it back together, just like they tried to put together the apple cart, but they will not be able to do it. For you are on the very verge of seeing great changes. For even before I come back again, and even before the anti-christ comes on the scene, I AM going to break the back of the anti-christ system. I AM going to start to do it now. Those who are in the high places are going to have a great fall. Those who control the finances of the world, those who control the governments of the world and the power behind the scenes, I will put to shame and will totally break. And who is going to put them back together? satan can't put them back together. The demonic can't put them back together. The principalities and the rulers of darkness can't put them back together. For Humpty Dumpty's going to have a great fall. And all the king's horses and all the kings' men cannot put them back together again.

For I AM defeating the enemy in this time. I AM exposing the enemy. I AM exposing the lies that he has told. Yes, I shall truly knock him out of the way. I shall back hand him out of the way. And then, even as destruction is taking place in the earth and even as they are fighting one another, oh, yes, after that, I shall move and there shall be a great shaking in all of the spiritual realm. For the kingdoms of the power of the air shall be shaken by Me and I shall upset them so; I shall disorient them so, and then I will come in with a move of My Holy Spirit that will truly set the captives free. For this is My time. And I AM going to have My way in the earth, and again I say that nothing shall stop what I AM getting ready to do. No financial system. No man. No government. No amount of money shall be able to stop what I AM doing. For I AM going to arrest the countries right now. I AM going to stop them in their tracks. I AM going to have My way, and then I AM coming soon, says the Spirit of the Lord.

- Humpty Dumpty is a character in an English nursery rhyme, probably originally a riddle and one of the best known in the English speaking world. Though not explicitly described, he is typically portrayed as an "anthropomorphic egg." Wikipedia.
- Anthropomorphic means described or thought of as having a human form or human attributes (anthropomorphic deities). Miriam Webster Dictionary.
- The Real Meaning of Humpty Dumpty as taken from Shared Heart Foundation. Humpty Dumpty was an egg! A symbol of fertility, creation, but also fragility. The complete life process. The entire DNA is there. The egg is also a symbol of the earth, which is not round but slightly egg shaped. Humpty was sitting on a wall, maybe just enjoying the view from up there. But there is always a deeper meaning to things. A wall separates us, but it can also separate two courses of action. And sitting on a wall can be like sitting on a fence, the

symbol of indecision.

- To see more, go to http://sharedheart.org/sharedheart2/the-real-meaning-of-humpty-dumpty.html.

Tip of The Iceberg

April 24, 2013

Glaciers.

A glacier is pure and clean and the water is fresh. A glacier is like the Body of Christ. It's pure. It's been washed pure by the blood of Jesus. A glacier is accumulated snow and ice and it slowly melts and it slowly breaks off into the ocean. And as individual icebergs break off and float out into the ocean, the icebergs represent the remnant people. And the icebergs are very dangerous, even as the Titanic was brought down by an iceberg. The icebergs break off from the main Body of Christ. You are the vanguard company that I send out. And the tip of the iceberg is sticking out of the water. And you can't judge that iceberg by how big it seems on the surface of the water, because the largest part of the iceberg is down under the ocean, where you can't see. This deceives many people because it's dark down there - and it's big and huge. But you only see the tip of the iceberg.

And in the days ahead you are only going to see the tip of the iceberg concerning what I AM going to do. For these icebergs that are breaking off like the Titanic, this represents governments. It represents militaries. It represents political parties. It represents corporations and even board meetings. And it is very dangerous. One iceberg can bring down a country. One iceberg. One member of the Body of Christ can bring down a nation. So these icebergs are breaking off and they are going into the ocean. And as these icebergs come out - these ships of nations and governments and militaries and corporations hit these icebergs - they are going to break up and there is going to be great destruction. And they are going to be brought down to nothing in the days ahead.

For these ships represent the deceitfulness of riches. They represent power. They represent man's grabbing every ounce of power that he can. But they cannot stand up against one small iceberg, the Body of Christ. So My remnant people, rise up like an iceberg! You may just seemingly be the tip of an iceberg, but I will use you to bring down nations. Even just one iceberg shall bring down nations and governments. And you shall wreak much havoc in the days ahead. For you shall be dangerous as an iceberg to the ships. You shall be dangerous to the enemy's work. For you shall bring down many demonic structures as they run into you in the days ahead. They will run up against something that is stronger than them.

For I have made you pure. You've been in the fire of oppression. You've been in the fire and the heat - but I have purified you. I have taken out the dross, My remnant people. So be like that iceberg that ran into the Titanic ship! Yes, you shall bring down the enemy's kingdoms in the days ahead.

Yes, you shall be just like the tip of the iceberg which seemed like brought down a great nation, brought down a great military, brought down corporations, brought down many things that are wrong. But look and see what I will do in the days ahead with just a company of people: the vanguard company, the remnant people. Yes, I will use the remnant people to change the course of nations in the days ahead, to change even the world. I will use the remnant people, the icebergs, I will use them to turn the world upside down! For they are stronger than they seem to be. And I AM saying today, you are stronger than you seem to be! So don't think little of yourself, because I have made you great! And you are great in My eyes. And the great power and anointing shall be manifested in you in the days ahead. And the world shall be in awe and fear of even My little ones in the days ahead. For they shall walk in My glory. They shall walk in My power and will do great exploits in the days ahead. They will do great things for Me and wreak havoc on the world and on satan's kingdom. They shall wreck his kingdom in the days ahead. MY people, that I have raised up for such a time as this! They shall be strong and do many signs and wonders in My Name, says the Lord your God.

These ships which represent nations and corporations and governments, like Titanic, were considered unsinkable . But one iceberg brought the Titanic down. Oh, yes, it only takes a little spark to get a fire going. So the enemy will be surprised in the days ahead. The peoples of the world will be surprised in the days ahead at what was brought down. One person brought down and exposed things that brought down a government or a corporation or a military or a nation or a political system.

For, yes, I have empowered you I say unto you, My children. I have empowered you with the Holy Spirit. You don't realize the power you have! It is a great power! It is a great power that I have invested in you. Even as you have sharpened iron against iron and steel against steel, and as you have sharpened the sword of the spirit, you shall go forth and conquer it. And with the word of God you shall divide the soul from the marrow in the days ahead, says the Lord your God.

Is Anything Too Hard?

April 25, 2013

I hear the Lord saying today is anything too hard for Me? Jeremiah 32:17. Even as I brought Israel out of Egypt, was anything too hard for Me? All through insurmountable problems, is anything too hard for Me? Is anything too hard for Me in your life today? Oh, you that pray here with Me, night and day, is anything too hard for Me to do for you? Even the small desires of your heart that seem so hard for you, is it too hard for Me? Oh, no! Is anything too hard?

For the church that is spiraling downward, and downward, in a downward spiral. And this nation is going downward, down, down in a spiral. And the other nations of the world are going down, down. But is anything too hard for Me? Can not I shake the nations? Can't I have My work done in the nations? Shall not I have My last move of God in the nations? Is anything too hard for Me? Can I not bring the heathen unto Me? Can I not call them unto Myself, by the work of the Holy Spirit through you? Is anything too hard for Me?

For, oh, if you would realize the power that you have and speak it out and pray it out and talk it out, and talk My Word, and talk about victory - is anything too hard for Me? For if you continue with Me the way I've called you to continue with Me, in prayer, in fasting, in seeking after My face, then things will happen. Then I will surely share My secrets with you for I shall share My secrets with you concerning the things which are to come and which will even soon happen in this age, and in this time, and in the world now, in this time and in this generation. I will share the secret things that are about to happen and how I AM going to do it with you, says the Spirit of Grace unto you.

War and War

April 30, 2013

War and War.

Oh, yes, events are starting to shape up in the earth for great conflict.

One smaller war and one larger war.

The destruction shall be such as you have never seen. You

shall pull back in horror. You shall be horrified at the sight and sounds that you shall see on the TV. It shall be horrific. But you shall know that My hand is in this. And even as My hand moves to protect Israel in one war, you will see destruction such as the world has never seen. But it must come to pass. It must come to pass, because after this shall be the great shaking. After this shall be the shaking of financial systems, economic systems, and of governments. For I shall shake several areas of the world, financially, economically, as well as militarily. And you shall see after this shall begin the great move of God that you have waited for. For this shall help to usher in the great move of God and then after this great move of God, where the souls of many shall be saved and delivered, the tormented set free, the captive set free, the gospel sent to the uttermost parts of the earth, to every tribe, tongue and nation, then I will come in all My power and glory; and I will catch you away, My saints. Oh, yes, the time is short, so labor and work for Me. The time is coming, you know, when you will not be able to labor, and all things must come to this situation. All things must come to a point, where things like this will happen. It's of Me. Trust in Me in the days ahead for I will protect you. I will protect you. Oh, I will protect you. And know that the end time days are shortened and you must work and labor for Me. Yes, the end time move of God shall be great. It shall come quickly, and then I will come, says the Spirit of the Lord.

The Die Has Been Cast

April 30, 2013

It will only be a short period of time because the die has been cast.

Nothing shall stop this thing that is coming.

Nothing shall stop it. It may be delayed for awhile, but nothing shall stop what is about to take place in the earth. For things must develop. Things must surely come to an end. All prophecy must be fulfilled. All the nations that are against Me will be totally undone in the days ahead. They will be totally undone. Leadership and all that would fight in a war against Me in the nations shall be totally undone. I will have My way. I will shake the governments in the days ahead. I will shake those that oppose Me. I will bring them to nothing, says the Spirit of Grace. So rest. When you see the shaking, when you see the governments falling, economic situations change, economies falling, banks failing, know that the time is short. Know it's of Me. I will shake all things in this last day, for I AM reshaping the earth to receive My Son, says the Spirit of the Lord.

Master Tool and Die Maker

May 03, 2013

I AM the Master tool and die maker. I cast you and I made you in My image. And I AM giving you the tools to work with. For I have given you tool of the Holy Spirit. I have told you what to do through My Word. The die has been cast through My Word. And the Lord is even saying today that in the days ahead, I AM going to put new dies in the world. I AM going to reshape nations. I AM going to re-tool, if it was, even an automobile maker or a maker of some component. Tool and Dies. And they have to be recast; they have to be redone periodically. So I AM going to re-tool different nations. I AM going to use the new dies to re-cast new nations and shape them in My image.

For even today some countries that are countries will no longer be countries, and new countries will rise up where they used to be. For this is a different time and a different season. And yes, I shall use the tools and I shall use the dies to change the world. For I AM going to change the governments in this time. I AM going to change economies in this time. I AM going to change the militaries in this time. I AM going to start to change the media and Hollywood. All throughout the whole earth I AM going to change in this time, for the die has been cast. And yes everything will be different than it has been before because I AM going to mold and shape this earth into the way that I want it to be. You were created, you were shaped and molded into My image. You were made intricately by Me. But those who have aborted My babies that were made in My image, I shall surely deal with and expose them. Those that are behind the wickedness in the earth, the great evil that has overtaken this earth, that grows worse every day, I shall expose them. I shall deal with them. Yes, the die has been cast and it shall bring a great, many changes.

Use the tool of the Holy Spirit.

Pray in the Spirit and you shall truly see the changes come in all the earth. For this is the day when I will have My way in the earth. Yes, I will even change, as it were, even the shape of the earth. Things shall be so much different in the days ahead. For significant changes in the earth are getting ready to occur in climate, in weather, and in many ways, many things will soon change in the earth. Yes, new nations shall spring up where old ones were. This is the day of the suddenlies, so every day will be a new day and everything shall be changed. The Lord says I AM coming quickly, but first I AM going to do some things. The die has been cast and you will wait and you will see just exactly what happens, says the Lord, thy God.

Times and Seasons

June 07, 2013

The times and seasons are changing right before your eyes. For soon, one season in your life shall end and a new season will begin. One time in your life will end and a new time will begin. One season in the earth shall end and a new season shall begin. One time in the earth shall end and a new time shall begin. For things shall not remain the same. For even as we get closer to the millennium that is soon coming, you shall start to see a shift in the weather, even, and in the seasons. And no, it's not global warming. And, no, it's not climate change. And, no, it's not foolishness of man. But it is My season and My time that is changing. For I shall start to shift things the way they were back in the beginning. For soon, nature shall start to change. Nature shall go back to the way it was in the beginning. Perfect. So you shall start to see the shifting. And, oh, it's nothing to worry about. It's nothing to be concerned about. For it is My shifting because I AM shifting everything according to My plan and My ways and My will. Yes, there's a great shifting coming in the earth. Even in the way we work. There shall be a great difference even in the way we work and conduct business. Yes, even in the way that churches worship Me. Even as the way they come together. There's going to be a shift. There's going to be a tidal shift. Oh, you think you worship Me? No! In the days ahead you shall truly enter into My kind of worship that I desire, for I shall teach you My ways. I shall teach you how to worship Me. I shall teach you how to come before Me in reverence and fear of Me. The reverent fear of God is important in the days ahead. And it will surely keep you as the shaking begins in the earth. Yes, the shaking in the earth is to change things back the way they were. For there is coming a shifting. There is coming a shaking. But I shall prevail. Nature even shall prevail. For nature is crying out for the manifestation of the sons and the daughters of God. And you shall come forth in this hour as My true sons and daughters. So My

Remnant People, I say unto you, prepare your hearts. Prepare your minds. But most of all your spirits. Prepare for the shifting and the change that is coming. For don't let it catch you unawares. Don't let it put you in fear. Don't let it put you in dread. Don't let it confuse you. For My time and My shiftings shall surely come. My time and My ways are different than your ways. My ways are higher than your ways. My thoughts are higher than your thoughts. Isaiah 55:9 So let your thoughts be conformed to Me. For the thing that is important in the days ahead is My Word. My revealed Word is the only thing that shall last. My revealed Word shall never pass away. Even the heavens and the earth, they shall pass away. But My Word will abide forever. Isaiah 40:8 So let My Word abide in you. Let My Words abide in your mouth. Speak them out and truly you shall see many great changes in the days ahead. Seek My wisdom. Seek My ways. Seek My knowledge. Forget the ways of man, for they are fast failing. For I am shifting things back to My time, to My ways of doing things. I laugh when I see the church services. For they are so far off what they should be. The worship is so far off. For, yes, I will show you how to worship Me in the days ahead. I will show you how to abide in Me. I will show you how to stay under the wings of the Almighty in the days ahead. For surely the time is coming when men shall not endure sound doctrine. 2 Timothy 4:3 But, yes, you will know My Voice. You will know My Word. My Word is everlasting and forever, says the Spirit of Grace unto you.

The Boomerang Effect

June 20, 2013

Oh, yes, you shall see those in the days ahead as they throw the boomerang. They throw the boomerang to hit the ankles of their enemies to knock them off their feet. The ones throwing the boomerangs are the news media, the governments, the banks, the stock markets, and those secret ones in the high places that rule the world. They have thrown their boomerang out, but don't they know the boomerang shall come back and knock them off their feet? For the scripture says, "Whatsoever you sow, you shall also reap." Galatians 6:7 And as one person has said, "what goes around comes around." So watch in the days ahead for those ones who have thrown out the boomerang, it is going to come back and it will knock them off their feet. For you shall see such a shaking as the boomerang comes back into Washington DC to knock them off their feet. As it comes back in the capitals of the world, as it comes in the high places of the earth, where these evil people rule; it's going to come and knock them off their feet. And then, My saints shall rise up and take the land, says the Spirit of the Lord. For this is My time and this is My season, and I shall truly disarm them with My own boomerang! For they have sought to do this in their own power, but I shall turn it against them and it shall boomerang back on them, says the Spirit of the Lord. So watch and see what I do, how I expose and depose in the days ahead. I AM just starting. This is only the beginning. And it shall totally unravel. The secret shall be out as a light for all to clearly see, and many shall be shocked at how they were deceived by these people in the days ahead. It shall be a tremendous shaking across the earth as governments, as financial markets and the news media are shaken out of their secret hiding places. The evil shall truly be dealt with by Me, says the Spirit of Grace.

Political Shift

July 08, 2013

The Lord says there's a shifting coming politically. Even from the right to the left to those people in this country in between, there's a political shifting coming towards isolation. For, oh, yes, in the days ahead, the United States shall continue to anger many people. They shall continue to lose friends. They shall continue to lose influence in the world. And the people in this country shall grow tired of war. They shall grow tired of involvement in the affairs of other nations. And, yes, the attitude shall be one of 'let's stick to our own business. Let's put our nose into our own business. Let's disengage from the affairs of this world.' For the Lord says there's a shifting coming in the days ahead, and the Lord says there'll be an attitude to withdraw, but the Lord says I'm in it because this nation shall become a peacemaker nation. And even as this country is more at peace with other nations, then I shall be able to once again send people out of this nation as missionaries. And the people will receive them because they'll see they don't have a political agenda. So, yes, the nations shall heed the advice of George Washington not to mingle and mix in the affairs of other nations. So, yes, there's a spirit of tiredness, of weariness, from putting your nose into the business of the other countries and of interfering in their affairs. So, yes, there shall be a great change in Washington, D.C. And the shifting has already started. And you shall see it more and more every day, and you shall see My hand move in Washington as I continue to expose and depose in the days ahead. For I shall begin to take this country back to the way it was. I shall begin to dismantle the socialist and the communist influence that has come into this country. And you will see that this country will start to go back to the Constitution. Yes, you shall see how they shall change the banking system and many other systems, even the IRS. I shall start to move in the IRS. You shall see many changes coming in the days ahead as you fast and pray and as you wait before Me. Yes, you shall see that hearts shall be changed; for a move of God is coming to this Great Land. A move of God shall change the hearts and thinking's of many people and many groups and many races that are in this country. Yes, their hearts shall be changed and they shall even go a different way politically in the days ahead even as they see all the wrong they have been involved in. Many Christians have even been walking in deception in this country, but in the days ahead, they shall have a change in their mindset. And they shall know that they have missed Me. And they will know they have supported an abomination. For, yes, I will deal with abortion in this country. I will deal with homosexual marriage in this country. And I will deal with the nations around the world that sponsor homosexual marriage and that sponsor abortion. Yes, there shall be a great shaking in those countries as I shake out the leadership in those countries. For I will not tolerate this in any form, says the Spirit of the Lord. So I will shift and sift those countries and those leaders that have supported this abomination, for it's a stench in My sight, says the Spirit of the Lord. So, yes, even as revival, even as the move of God comes to this country, there shall be a shifting even in the political, and there shall be a shifting back to the ideas of the Founding Fathers and you shall see the great change that shall come into the school systems; that shall come into the courts; that shall come into the Congress. And you shall see a tidal wave of My power and glory sweep over this country, and I will truly set many captives free and change those mindsets in the days ahead, says the Spirit of the Lord.

Unity

July 08, 2013

A spirit of unity. I shall bring a spirit of unity to this country. Where there's been a spirit of division, I shall break down the dividing walls. Against race, even as those ones who have sought to bring one world government influence into this country, the hidden ones that have tried to destroy this country by pitting one group against another, yes, I shall break down those dividing walls. I shall break down the dividing walls between the rich and the poor; between the black and the white; between the red and the yellow; between the natives and the immigrants; between all different people groups and education groups and religious groups. I shall break down the dividing walls and there shall be a ground swell of unity in this country and oneness of mind. For this country shall rise up strong once again. Yes, I shall move and break down religion and I shall bring a spirituality in this country, but it shall be the spirit of the Holy Spirit. It shall be the Spirit of Grace, and the Holy Spirit shall move in this country such as He has never moved before. Even in the Charismatic movement, even in Azuza Street, even in the Healing Revival. There has never been such a move of God which is coming, and even the angel is almost ready – that huge angel is ready - to blow that large trumpet over Philadelphia, and then it shall begin. For you shall even sometimes entertain angels unaware. Hebrews 13:2 Soon you shall see angels even come and manifest in the flesh in your midst. For the amount of angelic activity shall increase in the United States and throughout the earth. They shall even be bearing witnesses unto Me. Are they not ministering spirits sent to help the heirs of salvation? Hebrews 1:14 For I AM going to send you many ministering spirits in the days ahead to minister to the Body of Christ and to even personally minister to you, My saints, My remnant people. You are going to see more manifestations of the power of the Holy Spirit in your midst. You're going to have many wonderful experiences. You're going to be shocked at what I do in the days ahead and how I do it and how quickly I do it. For what the enemy has tried to accomplish to undo this country in 200 years, I shall turn it around even in a short space of time. So just only believe. Nothing is impossible, only believe. Matthew 17:20 Watch and see and look and continue to pray and seek My face and see what I shall do in this great land in the days ahead. For the move of God shall sweep you off your feet. Yes, it shall catch the enemy unawares at what's going on. He shall be surprised at what I do in this great land. For I shall have My way. I shall respect the prayers of George Washington and William Penn and others that I made a covenant with in this great land. Yes, I shall move in this land. The seeds have been planted and, yes, the enemy tried to bring up weeds and thorns and thistles, but a beautiful harvest of souls shall truly come in this country, and then you shall go around the world once again to bring in a mass harvest. Then, I will come in all My power and glory for My people; My dear ones, My precious ones, I AM coming soon and will not tarry. Praise Me for My great deeds in the earth. Praise Me and glorify My holy Name, says the Spirit of the Lord.

Grace

July 08, 2013

Grace. Grace. God's grace. Oh, God gives grace to those whom He will. Grace. Grace. It's unmerited favor, and He's going to give this country a little bit more grace. He's going to give this nation a little bit more grace. All because of the remnant people that have been pressing in and praying in this country. From the East to the West, and from the North to the South, throughout this great land, I have a praying people that have been seeking My face and that have been crying out for a change in this great land. So I AM going to give the United States a little bit more grace. Yes, I AM going to give many parts of the country more grace. So thank Me, thank Me, because I AM going to move in this great land. If you will humble yourselves under the hand of the Almighty, I will lift you up in due season. For My hand is not shortened that I cannot save and deliver. Isaiah 59:1 So as you cry out unto Me, I shall save and deliver this great land out of the hands of the oppressor. For I shall deliver this country out of the hands of the evil one, that the enemy of your soul has placed in positions. For their strongholds and their kingdoms shall fall as you continue to pray before Me: all the evil intents of the enemy of your soul. I shall dismantle His hierarchy of this country. I shall dismantle his systems that they have planned and that they have very skillfully put in place for the last 100 years. I shall undo it even in a short season, says the Lord.

For this is the time I shall remove, I shall expose and depose, I shall reveal the secret, hidden plots of the wicked in this country; of the Masons, of Illuminati, of the Skull & Bones; all the secret organizations that have plotted against this great land for hundreds of years. I shall reveal their inner workings and their plots and plans, and it shall be common knowledge among the American people what their evil thoughts and plans and purposes were for this country. For I shall undo what the enemy has tried to accomplish. He thought he was almost there, but he showed his hand too soon. So yes, I shall redeem this great land as My remnant people continue to pray and cry out unto Me and seek My face. Know that I shall move in this land one more time says the Spirit of the Lord unto you.

Chicken Little - The Sky is Falling

July 08, 2013

The earth is the Lord's and the fullness thereof. Psalms 24:1 Yes in the eyes of God the earth and all the people, the inhabitants, are as mere grasshoppers. Isaiah 40:22 Who is like unto You? Psalms 113:5 For the Lord says, don't be worried and don't be deceived about the earth. Don't be deceived about global warming. Don't be deceived about what the environmentalists are saying, for this is only a fraud. This is only a hoax. For didn't I say in My Word that they would worship creation more than the Creator? Romans 1:25 Look and see what's happening in the earth. Even many in the body of

Christ are buying into this deception. The Lord says be not deceived for I AM not mocked. Galatians 6:7 For the Lord says, yes, I desire that you take care of the earth. For I desire that you be good stewards. 1 Peter 4:10 I desire that greed would not be found in your midst. But, oh, yes, I knew what mankind and wickedness would do to this earth through their greed to obtain minerals and wealth out of the earth. They would pollute the earth willfully. Even the communists - even Gorbachav - and those who would seem to be the leaders in the green movement, are they not the very ones who've polluted the earth the most? For the Lord says be aware of the falsehoods. Be aware of the lies. Be aware of the hoax. For this is mass deception on a grand scale. And it is meant by the evil one to bring about a one world government. To put the nations under subjection to the anti-christ. But the Lord says I AM going to completely reveal this fraud. I AM going to completely show you where it came from. And I shall reveal the hidden agenda, says the Lord thy God. For, yes, I desire that you be stewards, but the Lord says, I have planned in advance and even as the days go ahead, you will not run out of oil. You will not run out of anything. And don't worry. I saw the wickedness of men and what they would do to My earth. But the earth is made by Me in such a way that it can renew itself. Even though it's been badly abused. In time, it always renews itself. But the Lord says don't concern yourself with this for this is just a fraud. This is just to bring you into bondage. But the Lord says, yes, yes, soon there shall be a new heaven and soon there shall be a new earth. So don't worry. Oh, don't you fret. Don't you believe the lies told by satan. Because I have everything under control. I've got everything under control. Don't worry about the air. Don't worry about the water. Don't worry about these things. Because these people would only try to deceive you. But be wary of this, My Body of Christ. Don't buy into this, My Remnant People. Be wary of this deception in the earth in this last days. There's great deception surely coming in the earth in many different realms and many different approaches. As the enemy is so sly, he shall try to come in many different ways. But know My voice. Know the Holy Spirit's voice in the days ahead, says the Spirit of the Lord.

The Cry of The Oppressed

August 01, 2013

Yes, I have heard the passionate cry of many people in the earth. Many oppressed people in many nations. You have started to see it happen in Egypt, Tunisia, Syria, and also in Turkey. And you have seen it happen in Brazil. You have seen it happen in many nations, even in Greece. It shall spread around the world. The oppressed and those shall have a passionate cry for freedom not only in the natural, but deep in their heart they want spiritual freedom. They're going to cry out in China. They're going to cry out in North Korea. It shall be an unstoppable thing as this great turmoil, upset and rebellion in many nations in the days ahead. For the old order shall be undone and totally shook up as I move. They cannot stop what I AM doing. For even as I move in the natural for this passionate cry of many people; I have hear their voice - even though they don't know Me - I have heard their voice. Because it says in Psalms, I hate the proud. I hate their oppressors. I hate those that oppress the poor and take advantage of them. Psalms 68:1 The weak taken advantage of by the strong. And, yes, in the midst of this rebellion, against the authorities, against the corruption, against the evil in the days ahead, I shall sweep through with My Holy Spirit and have a move of God in those places, too, says the Lord thy God. So I AM going to move in Turkey. I AM going to move in Libya. I AM going to move in Brazil like I have never moved before. I AM going to move in Greece. I AM going to move in many nations on the earth in this hour. For even as there is open rebellion against governments, I shall move in when they rebel, and I shall move with My Holy Spirit for revival and the move of My way, says the Lord thy God.

A House of Cards

Aug 02, 2013

This is the season of a house of cards. You've seen people that are idle build a house of cards. Well, many nations, many governments, and many kingdoms are like that house of cards, and they're going to collapse. They're going to collapse and fall. You see, I will start soon in the governments of Africa, on that dark continent. I will start with Zimbabwe. And I will make an example out of Zimbabwe. I AM going to totally undo all the corrupt evil, witchcraft governments in Africa. I shall start in Zimbabwe. I have heard the cries of My people in many African nations for I have a people in Africa now, and I AM going to really break the yoke of bondage over that whole continent. I will send many missionaries out of that place in the days ahead. For the apple cart is truly being upset. The house of cards is blown down by the Wind of the Holy Spirit. You shall see many royal kingdoms where I shall reach out and I will touch the children, I will touch the families, says the Spirit of God, for what they have done. Many of the Arab monarchies I shall touch them in the days ahead. I shall touch the United States and Great Britain and nations around the world that have touched the Apple of My Eye. Yes, the house of cards shall collapse. For this is getting personal with Me. I have put up with abortion. I have put up with homosexual marriage and I will not put up with it any longer. Where I've touched the nations in the past by My power and My glory, yes, this shall be a time where you will see that sin has consequences. Real consequences. And where nations have been touched before and peoples have been touched, I AM going to touch the leaders now. I AM going to shake the leadership up. Yes, you will see because of two reasons: abortion and homosexuality, and because of touching My people and dividing My land. You shall see it happen in the days ahead. There shall be a hush. There shall be a fear as I go through many nations and I break the back of abortion. I break the back of homosexual marriage. I break the back of anti-semitic feelings and actions of many nations. For truly it shall be a time of shaking of many nations. I AM going to touch many royal families in this time because they have much influence and they have been behind many of these things. So truly to the houses of monarchies in Europe, I shall truly reach out in the days ahead. For many of those people have been behind one world government and they have the anti-christ spirit on them. So I AM going to reach out and touch those in the high places. I AM going to touch the families of those hidden ones that rule the earth from behind the scenes. I AM going to really reach out in the days ahead and make My feelings known. They are going to know without a doubt it's Me. This is My season, and I AM going to move in all the earth. So give a shout to the Lord for He is coming soon, says the Spirit of the Lord.

Age of Gentiles

August 14, 2013

The Lord says the Age of the Gentiles is coming to an end soon. For things shall not remain the same. For you shall see many suddenlies and much change in the days ahead. But be not in panic, be not in alarm, be not in fear or dread, for these things must come upon the earth. For oh, climate change is happening but it's not because of global warming. It's because nature itself is going back to the way it was in the time of Adam and Eve. For all nature is crying out for the manifestation of the sons and daughters of God who shall come on the scene soon and shall change the course of nations. Romans 8:19

Yes! But I say unto you, be not in fear but great war is coming soon, even nuclear war is coming, where tens of thousands of people will die a horrific death. And, yes, in the midst of nuclear war, it shall even change the climate, for the sun shall be shielded for many days. For you see much climate change in the future shall be caused by the nuclear war that shall happen. The radiation shall spread and many people shall be devastated by this war. But Israel's enemies shall be defeated. For I shall not tolerate what they are doing to the Apple of My Eye. For the Lord says, I've drawn a line in the sand and I say, No more! No more! No more! So with this war, there shall be a different season in the earth. Some nations shall no longer exist. And other nations shall take over the spoils of those nations. For out of this war Israel shall arise to be a great nation and even with their new technology, they shall prosper in business. Even with their new technology, they shall rewrite the books of war and military science. For the Lord says soon a great shaking is coming in the very elements. Many earthquakes and many climate changes for soon you shall see the weather shall really change. It shall be hot where it should be cold and cold where it should be hot. Yes, the seasons in many places of the earth will really cool down. And many places will warm up. So the Lord says believe not the lie of the enemy for he would only use this lie of global warming to try to bring about a power grab. But the Lord says I see the power grabs of the enemy all around and I shall stop it. I shall expose much in the days ahead.

I shall expose the Federal Reserve Banking system. I shall expose the Masons, the Illuminati, and those ones that are hidden in the high places. I AM going to expose whole governments in the days ahead. I AM going to expose the leadership of many nations: those who sit in their high places all smug and they think they are a god unto themselves. I will totally expose satan's plans in the earth in the days ahead. And the power grabs shall come to nothing. For the Lord says My people shall grab power at this time. For My people are coming on the scene in the world and they are coming forth in great boldness. They shall walk fearless. They shall walk straight faced. They shall even speak to many government authorities and tell them, "you will do this, you will do that." They shall speak with great authority in the days ahead. Even as Moses and Aaron confronted Pharaoh, My Moses and My Aarons shall confront many Pharaohs in the days ahead. And the fear of these leaders shall be on their faces as they see My ones, My dear ones, My humble ones, walk in great power and authority with signs and wonders. For the time is coming when there is great change coming in the earth.

There's great change coming in the church for I shall root out the hireling. I shall root out those who have only been in it for the money. I shall root out those ones who claimed they had the anointing, who claimed they had My power, who claimed they had a relationship with Me, but they had nothing. I shall drive them out, even as Jesus, My Son, drove out the moneychangers. As He cleansed the Temple, I AM coming to cleanse My Church. Matthew 21:12 I AM coming to cleanse the governments. I AM coming to cleanse and lift up many and destroy many, says the Lord thy God for it's a different season. For the Age of the Gentiles is soon coming to an end, says the Lord thy God.

*POST NOTE:

The huge navy ships and aircraft carriers shall become obsolete because there will be weapons that will bring them to rust and dust in a short amount of time. The whole concept of how war is waged will be totally different, says the Lord. So many military systems that have cost billions of dollars will be outdated quickly because there will be very simple, complicated – yet simple and sophisticated systems that will be developed and that are being developed right now that shall make the way war is being conducted in even the last 100 years obsolete. The Lord says everything is totally changed and everything is pointing towards Israel as the great world power.

The Greater Works

August 18, 2013

My precious saints, you shall soon do the "greater works" that My Son, Jesus said you would do before He left the earth. He said HE would send the Comforter, the Holy Spirit, which would be your Helper, your Guide, your Teacher, and that He would lead you into all truth and that you would walk in all power and authority in the earth. John 16:13 So know who you are in Christ Jesus and the power and authority that you have and walk in it in the days ahead.

The days ahead are uncommon days and I call you to be serious about My work in a way you haven't been up until now. The time is short and I AM going to do a quick work and then come soon! Romans 9:28 I will not wait or tarry much longer! I long for My flock, My little ones. So you shall walk straight faced before man in the days ahead with great authority. They will know you are not afraid of their faces walking not as mere man, but as vessels of honor: My ambassadors to bring My Name to a wicked generation. You will be bold for Me and will not plan what you will say or do but only when you are face to face will I put My Words in your mouths. I shall bring you before the important rulers, kings, presidents, and you will boldly speak and some will want to hear you and be saved. Others, (the hidden ones) will tremble, fall down, some will even faint, while others will be shame faced. I will expose and depose world leaders in the days ahead. You will use the power I give you for My glory and purposes and not for personal revenge. There shall be many situations with the "Pharaoh spirit" and you will be like Moses and Aaron. You will have many situations like when Saul (Paul) went to the authority to witness and Bar Jesus the sorcerer tried to stop Paul and while filled with the Holy Spirit, he spoke to the sorcerer and he was blind for a season and the ruler came to Christ. Acts 13:5-12

You will live the book of Acts and most miracles shall be in the market place and government offices and the schools. I will have My way and My Holy Spirit will back you with signs, wonders and miracles. The "hidden ones" possessed by their master, lucifer, will have no power before you and shall flee in panic and fear and be a laughingstock before their peers and in their sphere of influence. So stay in the Word, prayer and even some fasting, and wait, wait, before Me for soon I will move in My power and glory. Yes, the wealth of the sinner stored by them shall become yours for My Work and your needs. Remember always, My children, to give Me the glory for that I will not share with another. Be faithful unto Me until My soon coming.

Shock Waves

August 29, 2013

The Lord says shock waves. Shock waves of war are soon coming. Oh, but more important than that are the shock waves of My glory, which is soon to come on the earth. For the Lord is planning on using shock to take hold of nations at this time. The ones that work behind the scenes that the enemy uses, they're planning many schemes to take power quickly. So there shall be shock waves happen all around the world. War, economic devastation, and all things they have planned for many years that they think they shall grab power sooner than they have imagined. But instead what they will get will be shock waves of My glory. In the middle of destruction, in the middle of all their plans and schemes, I shall send the shock wave of My glory into the earth that shall surprise many.

In Philadelphia, there shall be a shock wave of My glory. It shall be shocking to many people how suddenly things shall change in this city. Oh, yes, the shock waves of My glory that goes around the world shall cause whole situations to change seemingly overnight. Where there've been riots in the streets, where there has been destruction, oh, yes, I shall move in the middle of that. I shall have My way in different situations in the nations. And, yes, when it looks like the world is turned upside down, when it looks like countries are turned upside down, then I will move in that country. I will save whole nations in a matter of days and weeks and months. And the Lord says I shall change the course of history even in the time which is soon to come. For as you go into 2014 and 2015, it shall be a different time. It shall be a time such as the world has never seen. It shall be evil, but where sin abounds, grace does much more abound. Romans 5:20 And I shall have My move. I shall have My way. So the Lord says prepare your hearts. Get ready to move for My Kingdom and to possess territory for the camp of the Lord. For we are a mighty army, a mighty army of one. One Spirit; we are one spirit. We are one flesh. We are one with Him, for He bought our salvation. So we are one with Christ Jesus. Nothing shall be impossible unto you, if you only believe. Matthew 17:20 Ask for the impossible. Ask for the nations. Ask for the heathen and they shall be yours for an inheritance, says the Lord thy God. For the Lord says, yes, yes, take territory now. Take territory now. You have been taking it in the spiritual realm and soon you will see the manifestation of it in the natural, says the Lord your God.

That None Should Perish

August 29, 2013

I AM not willing that any should perish. 2 Peter 3:9 The Lord says, I AM the God of the second chance. The Lord says, I AM giving many nations a second chance. The Lord says, I AM giving Philadelphia a second chance. I AM giving Philadelphia a new life. I AM giving this country a new life. The Lord says, I AM not willing that any should perish. For the Lord says, I AM extending the time of My mercy in all the earth. I AM extending the time of My mercy for this country.

This country shall turn back to Me. In many cases it shall be hard and difficult, but then suddenly I will move and will break down dividing walls. Suddenly, I shall move and tear down the enemy's structures that for hundreds of years he has built up in this country. The Lord says, yes, I AM not willing that this country should perish. Because they have sent missionaries too many other countries. Because their ancestors prayed and waited before Me. The Lord says, I AM not willing that any should perish. I AM not willing that many nations should perish in a nuclear holocaust. The Lord says, I shall save many peoples in the days ahead. When it looks terrible, I will move in and save the lost. I will save the heathen. Whether they want to be saved or not, the Lord says, I AM going to move on them anyway. I AM going to so shock them into the Kingdom of God, says the Lord. So the Lord says prepare for the shocking move of God. Prepare for the looks on many people's faces as they come on TV and they don't know what to say or do: politicians, Hollywood, the news media. They shall not know what to say or do. But in the end they'll have to say, it's beyond us! It's out of our hands. It's out of our control. And the Lord says that's the way I want the church. I want the church out of the hands of the religious. I want the church out of the hands of the hireling. Out of the hands of the false shepherds. And I will take the church away from the false shepherds. I will take away the false. I will expose it and I will redeem the time in the church because of the evil days thereof. For I have a remnant people and they shall rise up across the earth in this hour and be bold and strong for Me. They have the spirit of Joshua. They have the spirit of Caleb. And they shall go take the land in this hour and I shall make them strong, says the Lord thy God.

Prepare for The Unexpected

August 29, 2013

Prepare for the unexpected. I shall even upset the enemy's camp. Some nations that seemed to be goat nations and that seemed to be in his camp, all of a sudden I shall upset the apple cart. I shall bring them into the Kingdom of God. I shall have a shocking move of God in these countries that you can't even imagine that I shall be able to move in. I shall move in these countries and the general public shall be in awe and in shock as they see situations turn around in some of the most evil countries in the world. Oh, yes, I shall have My way: a shocking move of God that will shake the foundations, that will shake the kingdoms of this earth. For, yes, it shall be shock and awe. Even as they talked about the wars in the past where they did shock and awe. Yes, I AM going to shock an awe the public. I AM going to shock and awe the enemy's camp. I AM going to shock and awe them right when they think they have tight control over the world, the financial markets, the people, the political scene, I shall have My shock and awe and I shall upset the apple cart. Yes, the apples shall be rolling everywhere. And I shall laugh at these ones that are hidden behind the scenes that have plotted these schemes, as they try to grab and try to retake the apples and use them again. The whole situation will be spoiled, for I AM going to spoil them. I AM going to spoil the enemy, says the Lord thy God. I want to take the fruit for Me. I AM going to take the fruit for Me. So the Lord says, in the days ahead when there is much evil, even when there's shortages and when there's lack, let your watchword be the fruit of the Spirit. So the fruit of your spirit: love, joy, peace, patience, longsuffering, gentleness, kindness, meekness – let it be your calling card in the days ahead. Galatians 5: 22-23 People shall know you by your love for each other. And by your love for the sinner and by your love for the unlovely, in the days ahead, that shall move them. The love of God through you shall move many people out of satan's kingdom into My Kingdom. For the Lord says Kingdom days are just ahead. So the Lord says your greatest days of blessing are just ahead. Your greatest days of My anointing are just ahead. So the Lord says, watch and pray. Watch and pray and see what I shall do.

Days of Crisis

October 24, 2013

Days and days of crisis. Days and days of one disaster after another. People are weeping and crying and hollering and shouting and in confusion, as there's one disaster after another. One crisis after another. For people in the days ahead will not know which way to turn, because it shall seem unending, one after another. One after another. One problem. One headache. One thing after another. Upheavel as the world has never seen. Even in disasters and wars, one crisis after another. Economically. In the government. One thing after another. You get up every morning and you are facing another crisis in the world. Another disaster in the world. There's too many to handle. There's too many to handle. There's not enough help. There's not enough supplies. Everything is upside down.

The Lord says, oh, don't worry, I'll be with you. I'll be with you. I'll preserve My remnant people. But it's coming. It's coming. It's coming. Sooner than you can imagine. It's coming. It's coming. So the Lord says, weep for the lost. Weep for the lost. Cry for the lost. Be in travail for the lost. Be in travail for the Body of Christ. For it shall catch everyone unaware. Unaware of what's happening, for the people will not be expecting it. The people will not be expecting it. Even the Christians will not be expecting it because they've been asleep at the wheel. They've been asleep at the wheel. The Christians have been asleep. Give a warning to wake up! Give a warning to wake up! For they're crying peace and safety, but sudden destruction is coming. 1 Thessalonians 5:3 And sudden destruction is coming in war and disasters. In one crisis after another.

The Lord says, weep before Me today. Wait before Me today. Know that you're under My protection. Know that I

AM giving you insight into that which is to come. I AM giving you information that few have. The Lord says, I AM really with you. I AM really with you. And I'll be with you even as we get close to the end of this age. I will be with you more and more, and I will protect you. I will tell you which way to go. You need to fine tune your hearing so you know which way to go and what to do, so your life, itself would not be lost. But fear not, for I AM with you to say go to the right and you can avoid disaster. Go to the left and you'll avoid that crisis. The Lord says I will tell you which way to go and I will protect you and your family, says the Lord thy God. For lo, I AM with you, even unto the end of the world, says the Lord thy God. Matthew 28:20

Rocking Like The Train

October 24, 2013

I see the wind blowing.

The wind's blowing and the ocean's howling.

The whole earth seems like it is on a rocking boat.

Even as I was on the train the other day and the train was rocking on the tracks.

It seems like the whole world will be rocking like the train was on the tracks.

Rocking. Rolling. Swaying.

Topsy turvy. Upside down. Helter skelter.

Running to and fro. Running with no place to run.

No place to hide. They're just going to have to hide under His wings.

Under My wings like the mother hen shields her chicks.

I AM going to surround you with my mighty angels of protection.

My remnant people, I've got a job for you to do. Before you do the job and before the move of God comes, there's war and there's crisis and there's disasters and there's calamity. There's everything under the sun imaginable that's going to happen. So don't be worrying about how it's going to be because it will be destruction. It will be calamity. It will be war. It's going to be many things. It's upheaval. The earth is heaving. All society is breaking up. Soon is coming a big war. Soon is coming a move of God. Soon I AM coming for you, My saints. Soon I AM coming in all My glory the Church will fall away. They won't endure sound doctrine (2 Timothy 4:3). Even after the great move of God, they'll start to fall away says the Lord. Know your doctrine. Remain steadfast. Don't believe a lie from the enemy. Don't believe the false doctrine that he will try to bring in the last days. The doctrine that would put you in bondage. Don't believe a lie. Don't believe a lie. Follow after Me. Know My voice. Know My voice. Know My word and stand on My Word. People will say, oh, that's for old times. The Word is passed away or that translation's not correct. Or this or that. They'll try to excuse it. But you will know My Word. You must know My Word to stand in the days ahead.

The Lord says I will make a way where there seems to be no way. Out of the wilderness. Out of the disaster. Out of the tribulation that is coming. I will make a way for My remnant people to escape.

Jack and Jill

December 05, 2013

Jack and Jill went up a hill to fetch a pail of water. Jack fell down and broke his crown and Jill came tumbling after. Yes, Jack and Jill, they're running up Capitol Hill to fetch a pail of water. The Jacks and Jills are surely going to fail in this hour. For they would like to bring this country down. Those that would like to spend and spend and destroy this country. The Jacks and the Jills as they're running up and down the Hill to steal and rob from the American people. Yes, I shall expose the ones in this country that would like to bring in the One World Government. I shall expose those even in the Treasury Department that would like to bring about One World Currency. I AM going to expose what's going on in Washington. And all the people in this great land shall know, they shall be shocked and they shall be ashamed when they know they have been deceived by many in Washington, D.C. In years passed, in days passed, in many ancient times even in this country. It goes back a long time that there've been plans to bring down this government. But the Lord God says Jack and Jill can run up the hill all they want to, but I AM going to break their crown; I AM going to bring them down. The Humpty Dumpty's I AM going to bring them down. I AM going to bring all those down and destroy them. There's not enough king's horses and there's not enough king's men to put them back together again what the enemy tried to do. For I AM going to bring down the enemy's structures. The Lord says it shall be a different time in this country. For I AM going to have My way in the government. I AM going to have My way in the Pentagon. I AM going to have My way. They can't push the Christians aside. They can't push Christianity out of the Military. They can't push Christianity out of this county. For the Lord says, No! No! No! They can't push Jesus out, period! And the Lord says, I've had it. I'll have no more. For this is a new season and a new time. And I AM coming with My sword, says the Spirit of the Lord. I AM coming to divide asunder the evil from the good. I AM coming with the sword, says the Lord thy God. I AM coming soon with My sword and I AM going to work in this country. I AM going to move in this county. I AM going to send this country out to the nations once again. But first, a great move of God in this country. First, many wrongs shall be righted. First, I shall expose the evil, and I shall deal with it, says the Spirit of Grace.

Days of Destruction

February 11, 2014

The Lord says days of destruction. Days of disruption. Days of disturbance. Days of disorder. Days when everything shall seem to be upside down. For even the way you shop. Even the way you travel. Even your mindset in the days ahead shall be different. For you shall have to prepare when you are going to do something major to go around all the obstacles that there will be in the nations in the days ahead. Truly, it shall be a different time and a different season than you have ever imagined in all the earth. Everything shall be more difficult. Everything shall be more complicated. At the same time, it shall seem to be simple in so many ways but there shall be a complication to everything that you try to do. In the days ahead, there shall be much disruption in the weather patterns. Even in the coming months you shall be surprised at what shall happen with the weather patterns. But know this: I AM here for you, My remnant people. I will protect you in the midst of the storms that are coming. There's devastation coming. Even terror attacks in this country for the enemy knows now where we are weak. And the enemy shall try to take advantage of every situation. And the Lord says, yes, there shall even be great disobedience in this country to the government. For the people have lost faith in this government. They've lost faith in all the political parties. Even our institutions, they've lost faith in. And the Lord says, it's so sad because they have lost faith in the Church. Because the Church has let them down. The Church has only taught religion and not a personal salvation; not a personal deliverance; not a personal healing; not a personal God that can meet your need and be by you and stand by you. But the Lord says, you must tell the people in the days ahead! Yes! Herald and Proclaim that I AM the Lord thy God that health thee. Exodus 15:26. I AM the Lord thy God that's your provider. Genesis 2:14. I AM the God that will never leave or forsake you. Hebrews 13:5. I AM the God that will always be by your side. So herald it out! Tell the truth in the days ahead. There shall be many hungry hearts and many hungry minds and they shall soak up and you shall saturate them with My Word. They shall soak up your love in the days ahead. So be saturated yourselves with My Word. Know My Word. Know My precepts. Know My concepts. Because the time is coming, yes, the time is coming when many will not endure sound doctrine. 2 Timothy 4:3. Many shall be led away by strange and seducing spirits. So the Lord says it shall be in turmoil. It shall be in uproar. Oh, but I shall move in the Market place, says the Lord thy God. Don't look in the Churches for Me to move for I shall move in the Market Place. Yes, I've said it before, that I shall move in the Military, in the Schools, in Business. Yes, I shall move and have My way.

The Lord says, there's a great shaking coming soon in the Financial Markets. A great shaking coming in the Global Currency Markets. In all the central banks. There's a great shaking coming in the malls, and even in the fast food restaurants. You shall see business turned upside down. For the Lord says, things shall be simplified in the days ahead. In many ways, things shall be more complicated but yet in a way they shall be more simple. For the Lord says, there shall not be the product available like it was before. For all the economy shall change in the days ahead and you will have to depend more and more on Me to supply your every need and to get you from Point A to Point B. Yes, I have a sure supply and My remnant people shall walk in My prosperity. They shall walk in My knowledge. They shall walk in My ways. They shall have the wisdom of how to operate in the days ahead. Yes, I shall impart unto you My wisdom of how to operate, and how to conduct business, and how to conduct the affairs of this life in the days ahead. And those around you shall be amazed at how you shall make the adjustment in the days ahead. For you shall make the adjustments in the very hard season just ahead. The Lord says things are just ahead, but yet a little while and you shall see My coming in all My power and glory. But first, a great shaking in the heavens and on the earth. A great turning to Me shall there be in the earth. For the Lord says, yes, soon world events shall take many by surprise. But they will not take you, My remnant people, by surprise. For I have prepared you in the fiery furnace of affliction. I have prepared you in prayer. I have prepared you in fasting. I have prepared your mind for that which is to come. So the Lord says soon a Great War is coming then a great move of My Spirit. So be ready, for I AM really going to take care of My saints, says the Spirit of the Lord unto You.

The Hands of the Enemy

May 29, 2014

The enemy's hands are getting ready to grab. They're getting ready to reach out. They're getting ready to grab power. Even before this election this fall, in November, they are getting ready to try to grab power. If you have eyes to see and ears to hear what the Spirit's saying, you shall see it in the newspapers and on the TVs. You shall know it in your spirit. You shall know that the enemy is trying to grab power at this time. And the Lord says, yes, as you continue to pray, as you continue to push, as you continue to believe Me, yes, I will spare this great land. I will spare this great country. For the Lord says, yes, the enemy, he's trying to reach out. He's trying to take away the spiritual freedom you have in the political arena. And the Lord says, oh, yes, as you continue to pray and wait before Me, I shall reveal who I AM. I shall reveal that I AM the Great I AM. And I shall move in this time, in this season, like I have never moved before in this country.

For the Lord says, I'm getting ready to show My Hand. Even the enemy, satan himself, would try to reach out and bring disruptions in business, in finances, in the government at this time. He would even try to stop what I AM doing. But the Lord says, I shall come in like a flood. I shall flood him even as it's been flooding lately. Even as there've been mudslides, lately. Yes, I'm going to flood the enemy. I'm going to defeat him with the prayers of My saints in this time. For the Lord says, greater is He who is within you than he that is within the world. 1 John 4:4. And let it be known unto you that the Greater One lives in you. And He's greater than the devil. He's greater than every situation that the enemy would try to bring into this country at this time. And the Lord says, yes, we shall have a great victory this year. In your ministries. In your personal lives. The breakthrough is even at hand. So the Lord says, push a little bit more. Be bold for Me. Be strong for Me. Be courageous. Take courage in this hour, for I AM with you. And My hand is not shortened that I cannot save and deliver, says the Spirit of Grace unto you. Isaiah 59:1

CHAPTER 5
PROPHECY CHURCH - JEWS

Yokes Broken

March 08, 2013

I have come to break the yokes over your lives.

I have come to bring deliverance.

Man cannot break that yoke.

Mental institutions cannot break that yoke.

Counselors cannot break that yoke.

It's only the Anointing of The Holy Spirit that breaks the yoke and sets the captive free, says the Lord.

Words of Comfort

March 20, 2012

Humble yourself under the mighty hand of God. Humble yourself and walk uprightly before Me in the days ahead. For the days ahead shall not be ordinary days. Yes, they shall be uncommon days. They shall be days of My glory that you haven't seen in the earth before. Many have longed to see this day, but you shall live in this day. You shall walk in this day. As you humble yourself before Me, and as you walk in the beauty of holiness, for I AM calling you to be holy, even as I AM holy; to walk upright before Me - yes, I will be your defender in the days ahead. I will go before you and the angels will be your rear guard. I'll make a way in the wilderness. Even in the difficult times, you shall see that My hand is not shortened that I cannot save and deliver. For lo, I AM with you even unto the end of this age. For surely, I AM with you; surely I AM coming quickly. Do not panic but be steadfast. For there shall be many trials and tribulations upon the earth in this hour and on the peoples of the earth. But My remnant people, My special ones I will hide in the secret place of My provision. I AM your provision, and I shall truly see you through all the difficult days ahead. Oh, how I shall shelter you from all the attacks of the enemy and all the things in the natural is up to Me. But I will send more angels into the earth in the days ahead, even to be witnesses for Me, even to protect you. And the Lord says, I will strengthen your feeble hands in the days ahead. Just walk upright before Me. Walk in the beauty of holiness. Be a holy people unto Me.

Tarry, tarry, tarry and wait for Me. See how I shall move for you in the days ahead. I AM your provider. Many things must be fulfilled before I come. There are difficult days ahead for the world at large, but I shall shelter you under the wings of the Almighty. So fear not! Your every need shall be supplied, if you'll only walk in faith. If you'll only walk trusting Me. Look not the right or to the left, but look straight ahead, for I AM looking right into your eyes, as you walk towards

Me. So keep walking on the pathway. For the way is straight and narrow. But walk you in it, says the Lord. Walk the pathway that is straight. It is even narrow – it is very narrow. And it is dangerous on the sides, if you would get off the pathway. But as long as you stay on the pathway and keep your eyes focused on Me, as long as you keep your eyes focused on the prize, on the high calling in Christ Jesus, as long as you walk it out, I shall be there for thee. I shall guide your hand. I shall take you step by step all the way to that glorious day, says the Lord.

Time of The Supernatural

September 26, 2012

You are now going into the season of the supernatural. Supernatural events in all of the earth, supernatural protection and provision. Signs, wonders in all the earth. I will supernaturally turn the tables on the enemies of Israel, the Church and move in such a way no one could imagine. I will surprise many, yes, even those who work evil and plan much mischief in this hour.

The next several months shall seem like eternity like you are on a roller coaster with the highs and lows. It will be a wild ride but hang on and go with me! Stay under my safe wings and abide in me and let my words abide in you.

Speak with great authority for I am giving you power, boldness and authority in the land. Be not afraid of their faces and I shall put my words in your mouth. For yes, you know these are uncommon days, but don't face them in dread and fear for I am with you my remnant people in this time and season. In this time of confusion and disaster, I will move by my spirit in a great way and without measure.

My Wealth!

March 11, 2013 3:40AM

The Lord woke me up early and this is what He very sweetly said to me:

I have been walking to and fro in the earth in the cool of the day, looking for you, My Beloved. 2 Chronicles 16:9 My Precious Ones, My Prayer Warriors, I AM looking for you to share My secrets with you. Deuteronomy 29:29 You have found great favor with Me and I will not withhold anything good from you. Psalms 84:11 Ask largely that your joy might be full! John 16:24 Many of My people believe I really don't want to bless them, but they have a wrong view of Me and some even have a religious spirit, but I want to bless those who have heard My voice and wait for Me, looking for the greatest move ever of the Holy Spirit. You have been faithful to wait before Me and to sit at My feet and learn of Me day after day. Now, I will bless you as you gather to pray, one, two, three, four, five; and I will share all that I have. The wicked in the high places have heaped up treasures for these last days, but I will sift it from them like grains of sand as it goes through their fingers and they will not realize how it happened. I will give it to you and others like you because I know and see your heart, your motives and feeling of love for Me. I will not withhold any good thing from you. Psalms 84:11 You will use it to finance the gospel and to enjoy yourself. I will take pleasure in it! Just continue to stay before Me in a humble way with a contrite spirit. I will pour out My blessings on you. Good health, secrets of My special ways, wealth, and the power of the Holy Spirit shall rest on you night and day. People will be in awe and even fear of you as you walk in the earth and they look and behold that you know Me and walk with Me. Because of your actions, I will draw all men unto Me. So lift Me up and again I say I will draw all them unto Me. John 12:32 Be of a clear mind and spirit, with a pure heart of love for Me and one another. I will now give you lands, houses, brothers, mothers, sisters, **with** persecution. I will send people to help you and they will serve you as I train them up to also be a special remnant people unto Me. Mark 10:30 Lands, houses, farms, factories, industries, I bring to you and put into your hands. So you will continue to do My will and My good pleasure. Use the wealth of the wicked wisely and take the gospel to the uttermost parts of the world! You even now will start to hear the sound of rain. After the rain shall come the great harvest of souls and I will separate the wheat from the tares. Matthew 13:30 This shall be the end of this age! The time is short, so labor for Me for I AM coming soon in all My power and glory for My Bride!

Right after this, the Lord said, put a guard over your tongue and your hand over your mouth. Think and be careful of the words that come out of your mouth.

This is connected under Vision to 'Angel with gifts' 3-11-13

Ananias and Sapphira
Acts 5: 1-16

March 25, 2013
The Lord is saying to me today as I pray that the same sin of Ananias and Saphira is in the church today and many are in danger. The Lord is saying, be ye holy even as I AM holy! Walk upright before Me and in holiness in the days ahead for we are almost in the new season that is the end time harvest and I will not tolerate what I have in the past. There is much adultery, fornication, and all manner of sexual sins in the church, which I will expose. The time has come where I will deal with it especially in the five fold ministry. The love of money and power and pride and all evil that goes with it. I will not tolerate it in this new hour. You will be surprised, My remnant people, and shocked beyond belief, at the ministries I will expose in the days ahead. It will be dangerous says the Spirit of Grace, to lie to the Holy Spirit about anything. You see, in the early church, it was not possible to lie or live a life of deceit, because the power and work of the Holy Spirit was so strong! Many today are like the scripture in Proverbs

26:14, which says they are like a hot, dry, wind blowing across the desert promising much, but delivering little! Don't make a promise you don't intend to keep, or you make the promise lightly to Me and to man. It shall be dangerous if you lie to the Holy Spirit because the work of the Holy Spirit will soon be like it was in the days of the early church except more powerful! There will be instant death! God will clean up and purify the church. As the Holy Spirit increases in these later days, (James 5:7) it will be impossible for anyone to remain in our midst with a lying spirit! The Holy Spirit's power and manifestations should be such as the world has never seen even in the early church. Great fear will fall upon those who see these things. Yes, I will take care of that lying spirit that has come into the church. Let your yes be yes and your no's be no's (James 5:12). Ananias and Sapphira caused Me grief because they lied and didn't walk in the God kind of faith. To the natural mind it seemed like a small thing, but check your motives and your heart, and obey only My voice. Walk in the Spirit and you will not fulfill the lust of the flesh, says the Spirit of Grace.

Body Coming Together

March 27, 2013

Things shall suddenly accelerate for except the time be shortened, no man would be saved. But this is a dangerous time in the earth. And every day shall be something different.

Every day shall be a new day - an exciting day - but don't worry and don't be in fear. Some days, your hearts will almost stop but the world at large, they will be in utter confusion. But you will know what I AM doing. You will know that I AM putting the puzzle pieces together. I AM putting the pieces together in your personal lives. I AM putting everything together. So the Lord says, Rejoice! Rejoice! For this new day is here almost. Continue to pray. Continue to seek My face. Continue to get a picture of what I want to do for yes, there are pieces to the puzzle that need to be fit together. You'll fit together all these pieces to the puzzle as you fast and pray and as you seek My face. One will have one piece of the puzzle. And another will have another piece of the puzzle. For this will not be about one man. This will not be about one woman. This will not be about one ministry. But this will be about the Body of Christ coming together. And all parts of the Body of Christ shall function together and be important. So the Lord says, it's a great work. And I say unto you today, workers together and laborers together; I'm the Head and you're the one that I have called at this time to do this great work with Me. So the Lord says, all the pieces of the puzzle in ministry, in business, in personal lives, I AM going to fit every piece to the puzzle. There's been a question in your mind and I AM going to fit them all together and you will be fully satisfied, says the Spirit of Grace.

Wheat and Tares

April 04, 2013

O taste and see that the Lord, He is good Psalms 34:8. For His mercy endures forever 1 Chronicles 16:34. His mercies are new every morning Lamentations 3:23. In this hour, He is extending His mercy a little while longer to the nations. He is extending His mercy and grace to the USA for a little longer. So now is the time to work and to labor for a time is coming when no man can labor John 9:4. Except the Lord build the house, they that labor, labor in vain (Psalms 127:1). I will build My house and My kingdom and it shall be great. No man shall be able to oppose it or stand against Me. Stand still and see the salvation of the Lord in the days ahead 2 Chronicles 20:17. I will protect My people and their work for Me. Except the days are shortened, no man would be saved Matthew 24:22. So I warn you what action to take. The spirit of the anti-christ is loosed in the earth and a great deception shall take place. Yes, there are more and more false brethren, but don't try to deal with them right now because it would damage the harvest. Let them grow up together, the wheat and the tares, and then when the harvest comes in, separate them Matthew 13:30.

My remnant people, be as wise as serpents but gentle as doves Matthew 10:16. Yes, My saints, redeem the time because of the evil days the world has gone into Ephesians 5:16. Amazing days like the world has never seen!

Breaker Anointing

April 04, 2013

The Season of the Breaker Anointing.

It's an anointing that breaks the yoke of bondage and sets the captive free.

Oh, yes! This is the season of the breaker anointing. For even the church at large does not understand the breaker anointing - or even My remnant people. Many understand the breaker anointing, but they cannot move in it. They don't know how to move through and press through. So today I say to you, oh, yes! The breaker anointing! Use the breaker anointing! Press through in the things of the Spirit. Press through to the other side. Break on through to the other side. As you pray in the Spirit, you will feel the press. You will feel the spiritual opposition pressing against you. As you continue to pray in the Spirit and proclaim and speak My Word and push through in the Spirit, then you will see the breakthrough that you desire. Oh, you will see the breakthrough that you desire! Oh! Oh! Oh! So break through today. You will know when you have broken through when you feel the release in your spirit and when you feel the heaviness gone. When the joy comes – when the laughter comes – then you will know. But even before you break through – even right now, start to praise Me for the breakthrough. Even before you see it, start to praise Me. For surely as you praise Me before you break through, as you pray in the Spirit, then you shall surely see the breakthrough manifested. And there shall be a great release in your spirit and you will feel refreshed and renewed.

So the Lord says, continue to praise Me, and the breakthrough for nations, the breakthrough for Israel, the breakthrough for the United States, the breakthrough for Philadelphia for the End Time Move of God is even at hand. So continue to pray in the Spirit and push through. Push past every force of opposition in the spiritual realm and then you will see the desired results and you will see My hand move and you will see it move swiftly, even in this time and season, says the Lord thy God.

Sit At My Feet

April 02, 2013

The Lord is saying today, sit at My feet and you will learn My ways. As you sit at My feet, you will learn of Me. You will learn My thoughts and you will go on into victory. So sit at My feet today. Talk of Me. Talk of My ways. Learn of Me. Learn by the Spirit the way to go. The Holy Spirit will teach you how to flow. So go with Me today. Sit at My feet. Move not to the left or to the right but just stay quietly with Me. Now let Me whisper My secrets to thee. Even as you go into the midnight hour, oh, the dreams and visions, they shall surely come out of this meeting today. For I AM with you. I AM with you, My Beloved. Come on in a little bit closer and hear My voice. Learn My ways. Know Me. Know Me. Hear My voice. I will take you a different way. I will take you a different way. I will take you a different way than the world is going. I will take you a different way than the world is going. For they are going off and many in the church are falling into the ways of the world. But learn of Me. My ways are different than the world's ways. My ways are higher than your ways. Isaiah 55:8 – 9 My ways are higher and different than the world's ways. Sit at My feet and learn of Me. I will teach you. I will teach you My precepts, My concepts. I will teach you My Word. I will teach you My wisdom. I will teach you to hear My voice. I will teach you to walk circumspectly. I will teach you. Oh, I will train you. I will send you forth. I will send you forth to the nations. I will send you forth into the nations. And I will give you the heathen for your inheritance. So come and go with Me. The time is short. Learn of My ways and My thoughts. Sit at My feet. Sit at My feet. Sit at My feet. It is wonderful to just sit at the Master's feet, says the Spirit of the Lord.

Honor Me!

June 03, 2013

This is to the Jewish people, but also to the Body of Christ:

What the Lord is saying is that you don't honor the Father, and neither do you honor Me. For if you had known My Father, you would have known Me. Moses wrote of Me and Moses spoke of Me. But you did not believe Moses so how can you believe Me if you did not believe Moses who spoke of Me? So honor Me and see My glory in the days ahead. But know this! There are many in the church at large that do not speak of Me. They do not know Me. They do not walk according to My ways and precepts. And didn't I say that you must honor the Father in heaven? But if you do not know the Father in heaven, then you don't know Me. But I will reveal Myself in the days ahead. Yes, you shall know Me in the days ahead and you will seek My face. For the Holy Spirit will reveal who I AM to the Jewish people. The Holy Spirit will reveal who I AM to the church at large that doesn't know Me, either. But you must honor Me. You must seek after My glory for in My glory is where I AM to be found. For I will honor My Father even as He has honored Me. So I would say unto you, seek after Me for the time is short. The time is short that you have before Me. So seek after Me and learn of Me. Learn My ways. Get to know Me. Honor Me. Walk in My precepts. Walk in My pathways. For the time is coming when you must know My Voice in order for your life to be even saved. So know My Voice in the days ahead when I say turn to the right or turn to the left or go to the north or the south or the east or the west. Really know My Voice. Really honor Me and glory in My holy Name, says the Lord your God.

John 5:39-47

God's Voice

June 24, 2013

God's voice. Hear God's voice. My voice. There's sweetness in My voice. My voice is sweet. My words are sweet. There's a tenderness in My voice. I AM tenderly calling unto you today. Yes, there's a sweetness such a sweetness in My voice. It's like the fragrance after the rain. Smell the fragrance after the rain. There's a sweetness in My voice. A tenderness as I call unto you. I call deeply unto you. Tenderly unto you. All who are heavy laden and burdened down with the stress and fear and worry and concern. I call tenderly unto you. For you're My little ones, My precious ones. Oh, dear hearts! My voice is tender for you. So run to Me! For My voice is sweet. My voice is tender. My voice is quiet. Be quiet before Me today. Be quiet in My presence. Be quiet as you go your way. Be quiet in your spirit. Be quiet today. For the world at large is loud and noisy and in distress. But unto you, My saints, My dear ones, I'm calling quietly to you today. Enter into My rest. Find joy in Me. Find joy and peace in that quiet place, as you stay before Me. Learn to listen to that quietness that quietness in My voice. Wait on Me. Wait in My presence for the still, small voice. For that quiet voice shall lead you in the way you should go. In the days ahead the Holy Spirit's flow. The quiet voice of the Holy Spirit shall talk tenderly unto you, telling you which way to go, which decision to make. Make that decision in the quietness of My voice. It's the voice of the Spirit. Learn to hear. Learn to hear that voice of the Spirit. IT's quiet. IT's tender. IT's sweet. Listen to that voice of love. For I have loved you with an unfailing love. Jeremiah 31:3. I sent My precious Son to die on that cruel tree. John 3:16. Oh there was love in the Son's voice. There was love in the Son's voice when He said let this cup pass from Me. Matthew 26:39. Let this cup pass from Me. But His love for all mankind - it overwhelmed Him. It overshadowed all the pain and suffering. He loves you in a special way. A never ending love. Jeremiah 31:3. Who shall be able to separate you from the love of Jesus Christ? Will mountains or tribulations by the way? Who can separate you from the love of Jesus Christ? Romans 8:35-39. Know today, there's love in His voice. It's the voice of God. It's the voice of the Father. He sent His Son. John 3:16. And the Son sent the Spirit. John 14:16-31. Let the Spirit's voice keep you in the days ahead. There's a dangerous period in the earth, but that voice of love shall keep you in the way. He'll teach you His ways. He'll teach you His precepts. He'll teach you His way to go. The voice of God is mighty in the earth today. Psalms 29. For He is speaking a new sound in the earth today. He's speaking a new word in this day in the earth, by the way. That voice is calling unto you. Learn at My feet. Learn at My feet as you sit tenderly before Me. The voice of God in the days ahead, it will even shout to you. It will shout to you. It will be loud unto you. It will warn you, but it's still that tender voice. It's still that sweet voice. It's not a voice of wrath unto you, but it's only a voice of warning unto you. It's a voice of warning that comes in love as you dedicate yourself to Me. That voice will steady you in the days ahead. For the evil days are all around you, so know that voice. Psalms 29. Know My ways. Know My precepts. Psalms 119:27. Know the voice of the Holy Spirit in the days ahead. For the voice shall tell you where to go and what to say. Luke 12:12. He'll even save your life, oh, by the way. It's a voice of the Spirit. And He's even speaking today. Go to the nations. Go to the nations. Be My voice to the nations. Be My voice to the nations. Be tender with the nations. Be tender with the nations. It's the voice of the Spirit telling you to go to the nations. Go to the nations. The voice is saying go to the nations today. For the time will come when they will not endure sound doctrine. 2 Timothy 4:3. But know My voice. Know My word. Know My ways. Take this gospel to the nations. So be My voice in the land. Be My voice in the land. Be My voice to stand for good. Oppose evil. Take a stand. Be My voice in the land. Be God's voice in the land. Let Me speak through you. Let Me be. Let Me be. Let Me be. As you yield to Me, your voice will be like Moses' voice. You'll have the voice and character of Aaron, even. Be My voice like the voice of Joseph and Daniel and the Hebrew children in the days ahead. The voice of Jeremiah calling out into this end time days. The voice of Jeremiah calling into the end time days. Jeremiah 38:20. So voice of God, oh, voice of God, speak to this people here today. Voice of the Holy Spirit, we call unto You.

Voice of the Holy Spirit, speak unto this people today. Speak unto Your remnant people today, oh, voice of the Spirit.

In The Beginning

June 24, 2013

....how things were in the first several chapters of Genesis. How things were perfect in the beginning. And even people lived to ancient of days. They lived a long time. But oh, yes, even as they walked not according to My ways, their longevity of life started to fall. And even today, it's very short. But as we go into the last days and as we go into the last several chapters of the book of Revelation, you will truly see...

So you see, in the first several books of Genesis how things were perfect. And even the longevity of mankind was amazing. But even as they moved and time went by, all the people and all the evil all the things they participated in caused the longevity to cease to be; and the time of their life expectancy was cut down. Everything changed from perfect, to truly more evil as the years went by. But as we go into the last three or four chapters of Revelations (chapters 19-22), you'll see that things will go back to being perfect again. And so, as we get ready for the millennium, you're going to see changes, you're going to see things start to change in the weather. Already you're seeing the longevity of mankind increasing again. Don't worry about the climate and don't worry about the things you hear and see about the weather and what's going on in the earth. For the earth is groaning for the manifestation of the sons and daughters of God. For as we get closer to the end of this age, things shall start to move back into the same way they were in the beginning: perfect. So know that My ways are perfect. Deuteronomy 32:4 Know that My thoughts are higher than your thoughts. Isaiah 55:9 And, yes, the only thing that will not change, the only thing that will not fade away is the Word of God for it is unchangeable and it will last forever. Isaiah 40:8 Even as heaven are earth pass away, My Word shall remain the same forever. Matthew 24:35 So know this! Don't be worried in the days ahead for things are moving towards the millennium. Even things are moving towards how they were in the first two or three chapters of Genesis. As we get closer to the end chapters of Revelations, you're going to see things start to go back to the way they were before. So look for the changes. These changes are good changes, and they are of Me. So don't worry or be in fear at the shaking and everything that is going on; for they are truly of Me, says the Spirit of the lord.

Word of Correction

June 26, 2013
UNITY
1. Oh, My children, be patient unto the coming of the Lord. James 5:7 For soon I will have you sound the alarm in

Zion. Soon I will have you to blow the trumpet in Zion. For oh, yes, at this time, put your hand over your mouth. For now is not quite the time to say to those around you that are walking in an ungodly way, that are not walking according to My precepts. I have called you to reprove, rebuke and exhort with all longsuffering. 2 Timothy 4:2 And soon I shall release you to blow that trumpet. I will release you to bring the correction. For the time is upon us when those around you - many will not endure sound doctrine. 2 Timothy 4:3 And I am sending you to reprove, rebuke and exhort with all longsuffering. 2 Timothy 4:2 But I say for right now, put your hand over your mouth for they will not receive it from you. But I say the time is even at hand when I shall send you forth to bring correction in the Body of Christ. I shall send you in and I shall cause you to separate the wolves from within the sheepfold. I shall truly use you in discernment, for you shall have a great discernment. Many times you will have a discerning of spirits come on you and you will speak My words forth in the days ahead. Oh, yes, the Lord says, the time is upon you when I will use you to bring correction and it will be received by many. Some won't receive correction, but many will receive correction. Many will repent of their ways and truly return unto Me. The Father's heart is one of wanting all to turn and repent and turn unto Him. 2 Peter 3:9 So I say unto you, soon I shall send you forth. Be as gentle as doves, but as wise as serpents. Matthew 10:16 I shall put the words in your mouth. It shall be sweet in your mouth but it shall be bitter in your stomach as you speak forth My words of correction. For I shall use you in a mighty way. Be faithful unto Me and I will make you a ruler over many, says the Spirit of the Lord unto you.

AUTHORITY

2. You shall walk in great authority. You shall walk in great authority in the days ahead. Know your authority in Me is great. Know your power is great in Me. For you shall speak to the winds and the waves and they shall obey you. Luke 8:25 You shall speak to the elements. And the Lord says I have placed that power and that anointing in you. You have more power, you have more anointing, you even have more wisdom than you realize. You have more power than you realize. Only know the authority you have is not in yourself. But only know that authority is in Me. So use it as I show you, says the Spirit of the Lord. For great days are just ahead. Dangerous days are just ahead. But they shall also be the greatest days of My glory. And you shall be the bearers of My glory upon the earth. You shall be the bearers of My glory upon the earth. And the glory cloud shall even rest on you and people shall know that you have truly been with Me.

GOOD NEWS

3. I AM the Glory. I AM the lifter of your head. For yes, truly in the days ahead, I shall use you to lift the heavy burdens off of many people. Even as you preach My word, be

instant in season and out of season. 2 Timothy 4: 2 As you preach My word, you shall truly be bearers of good news. It shall bring a healing salve to many people. For many nations shall take that healing anointing, that healing salve back to their nations. For I shall use you to help lift the burdens off of many people. For I shall put an anointing on you that you can take up their burdens, you can take up their cross. And truly you shall speak a healing word that shall really bring a help and a cure and a healing to many people in their mind, will and emotions, in the days ahead and even their bodies. You shall be one that I shall use to lift up My Name in the earth. And if My Name be lifted up, I will draw all men unto Me. John 12:32 So I will draw them unto Me and I will use you to help instruct them and bring them unto Me in the days ahead. So be faithful unto Me, My remnant people, My saints. Be faithful for the task at hand for I shall truly equip you for the job and you shall do it well for Me because of the work of the Holy Spirit in your life. So continue to let My Spirit work in you. Continue to let the fruit of the Spirit even develop more fully in you in the days ahead. Let Me have My complete way with you. Yield your complete will to Me in the days ahead that I might use you to the utmost for My glory, says the Lord.

The False Shepherds

August 01, 2013

Woe to you Scribes, Pharisees, Vipers, Snakes, Scorpions,

and all those False Pastors who rule over My churches with an iron hand all those that are hirelings. I AM going to remove you from your position. I AM going to remove you off the TVs. I AM going to remove you out of the churches around the world. Oh yes, I AM going to really move against you for you are unholy people. You are even like Eli's sons. You're like the evil priests in the Old Testament, yes, that I had to deal with. You're evil in My eyes and I will deal with you. I will take you out of your positions. I will bring you down and I will bring in My true ministers. Yes, you shall see it start to happen soon for you shall see the evil in the churches exposed. Yes, you shall see it in every church, totally exposed and naked before Me, says the Spirit of the Lord.

Homosexual Abomination

August 01, 2013

This is the time and the season where I will really deal with that homosexual abomination. It is perverted. It is sick, says the Lord thy God. For no, it is not a hate speech when you talk against the homosexual abomination. No, no, these ones perverted what I called them not to do with their body. I said for them to live in righteousness and holiness. So no, it's not a hate speech when you speak up for holiness and righteousness. But those in these last days, didn't I say that they would call the profane good? Yes, they call evil good and good, evil. Isaiah 5:20 For this is an unholy generation. This is a perverted generation. And I will not have Sodom and Gomorrah over again. So, I AM going to stop this thing. I AM going to stop this movement, says the Spirit of Grace. I shall shut it down. Yes, you shall see in the days ahead, there shall be a new plague among homosexuals. There shall be a new dread disease that will cause them to be quarantined and even separated from the general population for it will be highly contagious. And the Lord says I shall stop them right in their tracks. For the Lord says sin has consequences, and this is the wages of sin. If you sin and use your body in an unnatural way, then there's a consequence to it. So this disease shall spread and tens of thousands shall die from this disease. And I shall stop this movement right in its tracks, says the Spirit of the Lord. For I will have a people to walk upright before Me, says the Lord your God.

Post Note:

There will be new diseases among the homosexuals and it shall be as a modern day leprosy.

People will shun them and avoid them.

Let Me Wash You

September 11, 2013

Let Me wash you. Let Me wash you and I will make you white as purest snow. Oh, let Me wash you. Let Me wash you in My blood. Let Me wash you in the blood of the Lamb. Let Me wash you and I will make you ready. I will make you pure as the whitest snow. Let Me cleanse you and I will make you pure as the purest gold. For the Lord says, yes, yes, yes, I have made you pure as gold. I have washed you clean under the Cleaning Hand, the Scrubbing Hand of the Holy Spirit. So wash me and I will make you pure and white as snow. So the Lord says yes, you're pure as translucent gold. For the Lord says, you're fit for the Master's use. 2 Timothy 2:21 The Lord says, because you're clean before Me, I shall truly use you. I shall truly use this ministry in the days ahead. Even when there's failure on every hand, and when there's disasters and nightmares in everybody's minds, the Lord says, yes, I shall be with you through the storms. I shall be with this ministry through the storms. I shall be with you through your personal affairs, says the Lord thy God. For that which is coming is terrible. That which is coming shall even shake the confidence of My elect. But the Lord says, let not your confidence be shaken. Let not your faith be shaken. But the Lord says, believe in Me for I know the beginning from the end. Isaiah 46:10 I AM the Beginning and the End. The Lord says I AM the Alpha and the Omega the Beginning and the End. Revelations 1:8 And the Lord says, draw nigh unto Me and I will draw nigh unto thee. James 4:8 In the tough times and in that which is to come, draw nigh unto Me. For I AM your Provider. For I shall provide for this ministry. I shall provide for your needs. The Lord says prepare ye the way of the Lord. I AM coming soon. But the Lord says there shall be a great harvest. There shall be drastic results. There shall be a great supply coming to the Body of Christ, as I shake out the gold and the silver out of the world's and out of the enemy's pockets. I shall shake it out and put it in your hand, says the Lord thy God. For there's a sure supply in the earth. There's plenty. There's plenty with Me. I don't have a short supply. But the Lord says, you shall see, even as you pray and push through, the manifestation shall surely come. Drastic changes coming into your lives, even as drastic change is coming into the world. Drastic change for good is coming into your life. So fear not! For when there is no supply and when you see those around you with nothing, I have a sure supply for you says the Spirit of the Lord.

Coming Soon To a Theatre Close To You

September 12, 2013

The Holy Spirit says coming soon to a theatre close to you: It's Jesus Christ. But He's not a super star. He is THE Star. And all the world is His theatre. And then the Lord is saying that the earth is His footstool. Matthew 5:35 Oh, the Lord is coming and all the earth is His theatre. The enemy shall be sitting below His footstool and His feet shall be resting on that footstool. So the Lord says, rest with Me because I AM coming soon. And the whole earth is the stage and I AM setting My Return. It is almost ready. For the people are working. The angels are even working behind the set of the theater for My soon return! They're putting everything in place. The Greatest Show of All Time shall soon be. And it is just titled, "Jesus." Jesus. He's not a super star. He is THE Star. He's the Lily of the Valley. He's the Bright and Morning Star. Revelations 22:16 The Lord says all the earth is waiting patiently for the show. And the Lord says I AM going to show up just at the right time. I won't be late for My own show. I will be there in the theater right on time. So persevere. Press in there. For soon you shall see the greatest show ever! And it shall have action. And it shall have fireworks. And it shall have passion. And it shall have love. It shall have peace. And it shall have victory. So the Lord says today, victory in Jesus, my Savior forever. He bought me with His precious blood. And He sought me when no one else would. So He's the Master. He's the Master Actor and He's coming on the scene soon. So the Lord says, prepare your hearts. Oh, prepare your hearts for the Greatest Show of All Time is soon just at hand. For world events shall take many by surprise. But the Lord says everything must play out. Everything must play out in the earth. The whole show must go on and then for the finale, I will come in all My Glory for all the world to see. So the Lord says rest in Me today for I AM coming soon. It's just around the corner – the move of God and what I AM going to do in your life. So the Lord says, be encouraged. I AM going to move in your situation soon. I AM concerned about each and every thing in your life be it small or be it great. I have a plan for your life and I AM going to work it out. So the Lord says be patient unto the coming of the Lord. James 5:7

I Will Make a Way

October 03, 2013

The Lord says, I will make a way where there seems to be no way. I shall make a way where there seems to be no way. Even the ministries represented here. I will make a way where there seems to be no way. If you shun the evil and do the right, and walk in holiness and uprightness before Me, then I will make a way for you in the days ahead. In the middle of famine, in the middle of destruction, in the middle of financial failure, I shall make a way. If you do what is right and if you avoid the evil, if you'll walk in holiness and uprightness before Me, I will make a way for you in the desert. I will bring streams of water through the desert place that you are walking through, says the Lord thy God. For I AM really with you at this time. And you see, everything has changed. It's a new season. It's a new book in the history of the earth. Everything has now changed and it's a new beginning.

For some, it shall be evil and some it shall be a blessing. For My remnant people, it shall be a blessing. So walk in this blessedness that I have called you to walk in. Walk in this holiness and uprightness that I have called you to walk in. For the Lord says consider not the situations and circumstances, consider not your finances, consider not where you are today, but look unto Me. I AM the Author and Finisher of your faith, who for the joy that was set before Me endured the cross. And the Lord says, you've endured many crosses, you've endured many tests and trials, but the Lord says I AM the One Who delivers. I AM the One Who sets the captive free. I AM your Provider so look not to the right or to the left. Look not to man. Don't even think or imagine how it could be. For the Lord says, if you'll avoid the wrong and if you would follow after Me, know that I shall surely make a way, I shall surely make a stream in the desert for you in the days ahead. Know My Voice and follow My ways. Follow after My Word. Follow after My precepts. Follow after My concepts and My doctrine. Follow after the Word and let the Holy Spirit lead you and I shall truly guide you in the way that you should go. For the world shall holler and shout one way and be in panic. But go not that way. But go the way that the Holy Spirit shall guide and counsel you and lead you in, says the Spirit of Grace unto you.

Ministry Leader

October 18, 2013

For the new day that you're praying for the Lord says it is even at hand. For the Lord says I AM doing a quick work in this ministry (Capstone Legacy Foundation) and the Lord says you will be surprised at how fast I raise up this ministry to the place that I have called it to be. It shall be a catalyst. It shall be a leader. It will lead many and many shall look to this ministry to see how it is done. For the Lord says, I have saved this time for this ministry. And the Lord says, Redeeming the time because of the evil days thereof. Ephesians 5:16 Where this ministry has been pushed aside, there shall be retribution, says the Lord thy God. I will repay. I will repay this ministry, says the Lord thy God. For your faithfulness, I will repay you all - everyone involved in this ministry - for your faithfulness. I will repay you abundantly.

For this is the time to really catapult out into the thing that I have called you to be and to do, says the Lord thy God. For surely I shall shake this region and this nation and many nations. Yes, this ministry shall influence and prosper many ministries. You shall plant seeds into many ministries and they shall grow up and be fruitful. This is the time you have looked for. This is the time you have trusted Me for. And now I shall do it. This is My cry: Souls for My Kingdom! Souls for My Kingdom! It's harvest time. It's harvest time. Its harvest time, says the Lord, so continue to wait before Me. This is an important time in the earth. From this point forward you shall see as you go into the beginning of sorrows, as you go into the beginning of sorrows and as you see Jacob's trouble, in Israel, you shall know this is the time of the great outpouring of My Spirit, when I shall pour out My Spirit on all flesh.

Watch and see how I orchestrate everything, and how I put it together for you shall be surprised, says the Lord thy God.

Hold on I'm coming. Hold on I'm coming. Every need

shall be supplied.

The work shall be quick. My anointing shall overwhelm many groups of people. For I shall break down resistance. I shall break down that spirit that would exult itself against Me on the Main Line. The Lord says these campuses, I shall move in them. And I shall use Transformations. I shall use the IC Movement. And you shall be surprised at how I will orchestrate it for it shall be something that shall be out of the control of the universities. The universities cannot stop it. The administration cannot stop it. For I shall sweep these campuses, says the Lord thy God. Up and down Route 30. In and out of every lane. I shall do it. I shall do it. And I shall deal with that intellectual spirit. I shall break it. For I shall move on the campuses, say the Lord thy God.

So take the gospel to many nations. They shall be strong in Me. You will see the astonishment on people's faces when they see classrooms closed for days at a time and people on their faces before Me. Yes, it shall surely be. For this is My hour and this is My time and they shall not steal the education systems that I set up for Me, says the Lord thy God. For even as I started Yale for Me and Princeton for Me, they shall return to Me says the Lord thy God. For I AM coming in a different light. I AM coming as the King of Kings and the Lord of Lords and nothing shall stand in My way at this time. For this is My time and this is My day. The Lord says to set aside the sins that would so easily beset thee. Set aside everything and set aside much time for Me says the Lord thy God.

In the next two or three months, set aside much time and learn of Me and know My voice. The Lord says, fine tune your hearing for you shall need to hear Me very closely and very definitely in the days ahead. So fine tune your hearing of My Voice, says the Lord thy God. Know My Voice in the days ahead. For it shall be very important says the Lord thy God.

The nations are in travail. The nations wait for their Savior. The nations wait for their soon coming King. The nations are waiting for the good news of the gospel. How beautiful your feet will be. How pure your feet will be to them as you present My simple gospel and the blood of Jesus shall surely shine for thee. As you go forth from here, the blood of Jesus will shine for thee. And you shall win many to Me. For you shall be wise in the way you operate into the things of the Spirit. For I shall show you My ways. For I have a way. I have a key that unlocks the doors to many people's hearts, says the Lord thy God. And I shall reveal it to thee. I will show you how to open the doors to their heart. For hard hearted hearts shall be broken in this hour. I shall move on some strong men in this hour and they shall cry out as lost men unto Me. And surely I shall move in them and bring them tenderness, says the Lord thy God.

Stay in My Presence

October 18, 2013

As you continue to stay in My Presence in the days ahead, as you continue to stay and be caught up in the Glory Cloud, as you stay in My presence, then you will hear it just a little. And then you will hear it louder, til it will soon be overwhelming as you hear My hand hit the oceans. And you hear the oceans roar. As you hear My voice, as you hear My shout, as you hear Me holler and speak out into the world. As you hear My words, they shall impact the world. They shall impact Kingdoms and rulers. They shall impact in the days ahead. As you stay in My presence, you are going to hear My voice and know My voice and what I AM saying.

And the Lord says I AM going to intervene more in the affairs of men. No longer will I stand aloof. No longer will I stand off hiding in the shadows. But I AM going to come in right now and I AM going to show Myself strong. And I AM going to make My presence known in the earth so man cannot deny that I exist. For I AM going to intervene in the affairs of men. I AM going to move in such a way that I shall change Kingdoms and leaders and countries.

The Lord says, no longer shall I tolerate what they're doing in North Korea in the prisons to My people. And Red China to the people in prison. And Vietnam. And Cambodia. No longer shall I tolerate what's being done to My remnant people in Burma and around the world. No longer shall I tolerate what they've done in the Arab and Muslim countries to the remnant people. No longer shall I tolerate what they have done to the Apple of My Eye. For I shall destroy those nations that shall come up against Israel. You shall see it happen. It shall be shocking as the world sees in the days ahead what I shall do for My people. My remnant people who have stayed in My presence. I shall give them overcoming power. I shall give them great power and authority in the earth. For I'm coming in a different manner. For the Lord says we are almost at the end of the Church Age. The Age of the Gentiles is almost ended.

And the Lord says I AM coming with a voice and a shout of the Archangel. I AM coming with a cry. I AM coming in a different manner than I have come before. I AM going to make My presence known in the earth. With signs, wonder, and miracles, it will be without dispute Who I AM. I AM the Great I AM. And I AM getting ready to have My way in the earth.

So the Lord says, stay in My presence. Prepare your heart. Prepare yourselves to see the greatest move of God. The greatest manifestation of My power and glory. Stay in My presence. That's where you belong. Stay before Me, and see what I will do. For I AM the Soon Coming King. Lord of lords and King of kings. The Lord says, I AM coming soon. I AM coming soon. So wait for Me. I will not delay, says the Spirit of the Lord.

Days of The Supernatural

November 06, 2013

Days of the supernatural like you can't even imagine. You can't imagine how many of My remnant people I will use in unusual ways by the Holy Spirit in the days ahead. For yes, I told you even in the midst of destruction and chaos and disasters, I would move by My Spirit. And even though flights will be stopped in some cases and it shall be difficult to travel, the Lord says, nothing is impossible with Me. For in the days ahead, I shall even transport some of My people in the night time to other countries. And they shall, even the next day, think it was only a dream. Then they shall find a coin from that country in their pocket. Or they shall find dirt from that country on their shoes. But the Lord says, I shall transport many of My people in the days ahead when it is difficult to fly and difficult to travel. I shall transport them to other countries to preach. Some shall appear before important people in a meeting. Some in the jungle. Some in unusual places. And you'll even speak their languages. Supernaturally, you will speak their languages and preach Jesus and Him resurrected, and Him crucified. The resurrected Jesus Christ you will preach to these people and you'll see a mighty move of God. Think it not strange how the Spirit shall move in the days ahead. For how the Spirit moves and how the Spirit flows, nobody knows! But the Holy Spirit shall go with you and you shall flow in the days ahead like you would never imagine!

Think it not strange the angels will go with you and they'll even prepare a meal for you and feed you as you travel. And the next day you won't even be tired! And the next day it shall all seem as a dream to you. And the Lord says there shall be many signs and wonders in the days ahead. It shall be different. Don't imagine how it shall be. It will just come supernaturally to thee, says the Lord thy God.

So the Lord says, prepare your hearts for important days are just around the corner. Prepare your spirit, soul and body, for the thing that I have for you. For there shall be great days in the middle of turmoil. In the middle of confusion, yes, I shall move by My Spirit in the nations. And the Lord says, yes, soon great destruction is coming. Great War is coming. But the Lord says, I shall move you in and out of many countries in the days ahead. As well as bringing people to Philadelphia, I shall move My remnant people in to the nations. Think it not strange how the Holy Spirit shall move. Get ready for a Holy Spirit explosion. Supernatural explosion. Signs. Wonders. Miracles. And gifts of the Spirit in manifestation in the days ahead. So get ready to go with Me. Get ready to travel for Me, says the Spirit of the Lord!

My Father's House

November 08, 2013

So come and go with Me to My Father's house. Come and go with me to your Father's house. Soon I will catch you away, My little ones, My bride. I will catch you away into the heavens, where you shall abide. But before that, says the Lord thy God, there shall come a great move of My Spirit in all the earth. One last revival. One last time when I will move. For I AM not willing that any should perish but that all should come into the Kingdom of God. 2 Peter 3:9

I AM giving many nations, many peoples, many tribes and many tongues one last chance. So I shall sweep across the nations with My Holy Spirit's power. I shall sweep and minister and whole nations shall come to Me in a matter of weeks and months. Think it not strange how it shall be, for I shall surely do it says the Lord thy God. You will know that I have done it and I will receive the glory.

And the Lord says things shall be very different in the days ahead. Yes, war, destruction, and more earthquakes. More famine is coming. Great War and destruction is coming like the earth has never seen. But in the midst of devastation, in the midst of tragedy, I shall move and I shall have My way with the nations. The Lord says continue to support Israel and to pray for the peace of Jerusalem, for the Apple of My Eye. Psalms 122:6 For the Lord says, My hand is not shortened that it cannot save and deliver. Isaiah 59:1 And the Lord says, Ask of Me for the heathen for your inheritance and I will truly give it to you. Psalms 2:8

For the Lord says soon I AM coming and I AM calling you away to My Father's house. Say I'm going to My Father's house, where there's peace, rest and joy.

Changes

November 27, 2013

Changes. Changes. Changes.

Such changes are coming in all the earth. And the Lord says, I would have you, My remnant people, to know that great change is coming into your life even the way you see yourself. For right now you don't see yourself very strong. You don't see yourself very powerful. You don't see yourself doing great exploits for Me. But you see yourself as the world sees you as weak and as ineffective. But the Lord says, you're more ready than you think you are. You're stronger than you think you are. You're going to be amazed at the looks on people's faces when they see you walk in the room. They're going to sense something different about you. You're going to walk in great power and boldness. You're going to even raise the dead. You're going to be surprised at the things you're going to do but in some instances, they'll come to a point where they'll almost seem normal to you. And it shall be normal. It shall be the new normal.

The days ahead shall be very different. They're days of change. They're great days. Some days shall be like it was in the 40s, 50s, and 60s. Some days shall be full of peace and you'll think that you've gone back in time. And then the next day, the most horrendous things will happen and shock you. Things shall happen in the world that you can't even believe. It shall be a time of uncertainty. The only thing that shall be certain in those days is Me. The Rock, Christ Jesus is the only thing certain.

For, yes, the tide shall turn and change shall surely come. And, yes, I've appointed you for such a time as this. And they shall be afraid of your faces. And you shall walk in great boldness and demonstration of My power throughout all the earth. Yes, My remnant people, you shall take care of the religious. You shall go in and speak to them even as Jesus went among the moneychangers. John 2:14 You shall speak boldly to the religious. You shall condemn them for what they're doing in days ahead and challenge them to walk holy and upright before Me. You shall give them a chance to repent of their sins and of their evil living and of their thoughts and of their deeds.

But the Lord says, I AM calling you to rebuke and to exhort with all longsuffering. 2 Timothy 4:2 And the Lord says, you shall be gentle as lambs but you shall be wise as serpents. Matthew 10:16 And the Lord says, I shall make you wise in the days ahead against all the plans and the plots of the evil and the anti-christ spirit; and you shall have insight and you shall have such discernment. For the Lord says, yes, great days of change are coming. But you will not be caught unawares. But you will know My times. You will know My season. 1 Thessalonians 5: 1-11 You will know in an instant what to do in very dangerous situations. You will not have to weigh out this and that. You will know instantly which way to go, which way to turn. You will know My Voice like you've never known it before. It shall become so easy. Where in the past you've said, oh, it's so difficult for me to hear the voice of God. My Voice is going to be so plain and clear to you in the days ahead. You will know My Voice. You will know My ways. You will understand My thoughts. Even though My thoughts are different than your thoughts, you're going to come to a point where you shall start to understand My ways and the way I think and the way I do things.

For the Lord says, it shall be a different time in all the earth. Yes, rejoice! Rejoice! For there shall be many great days of victory in the midst of what the enemy would try to do. You shall walk in victory and uprightness before Me. The Lord says, yes, I'm shortening even the days because even the very elect can be deceived. Matthew 24:24 Yes, I AM shortening the days or the whole earth would be destroyed. For the Lord says, yes, I AM coming soon. But before I come shall be great days of joy in your camp and great days of victory. For, yes, I AM shaking all the earth. But I shall start My end time move in Philadelphia. I shall move around the world. You shall be surprised at how quickly it shall come. Yes, they're talking peace and safety but sudden destruction is coming says the Lord your God. 1 Thessalonians 5:3

I Am Coming Soon

November 27, 2013

I AM coming soon.

I AM coming soon in all My power and glory and in all My might.

I will demonstrate My holiness. I will demonstrate My power for all the world to see. Yes, I AM coming sooner rather than later, because the Lord says, if I didn't come soon, the whole earth and all of mankind would be polluted and destroyed.

So the Lord says, Great War is coming. Great destruction. Great famine. Great pestilence is coming. Disease, the likes that you have never seen. A mighty shaking even in the heavenlies. A might shaking on the earth. Everything that your imagination can imagine will happen in the days ahead regarding the weather. The Lord says, yes, first a big war then the move of God. But I AM coming soon because the hidden ones, yes, as they would try to taint the genetic make-up of the food supply. And, yes, even as the fallen angels are mingling and trying to produce a hybrid race, like in the days of Noah, yes, anything that they can imagine and anything that the wicked people on earth can imagine shall not be impossible for them to do......even the Tower of Babel. They can even go in space ships to the very heavens.

But the Lord says, the heavens belong to Me. Psalms 115:16 They cannot go there. They Lord says, yes, the fallen angels are once again mingling with humanity to change the genetic and DNA code of the people of the earth. The Lord says I must come quickly or else I must once again destroy the earth and all the inhabitants. The Lord says I will not have it. I will not have it. It is as in the days of Noah. It's in the days of Sodom and Gomorrah. And the Lord says, I AM going to do a great work. And then I will not tarry but I will come quickly for My people, My remnant people. I will come in all My power and glory. I will show the world who I AM.

So you shall see in the days ahead many signs and wonders shall follow you. And there shall be a fear and there shall be a dread in all the earth as they see My remnant people coming. For you shall walk in great power and in great boldness. But the Lord says, be not in fear. Be not in worry. I will show you ahead of the things which are to come. I will protect you. I will provide for you in the days ahead. The Lord says, yes, a great move of God and then I AM coming. Look for Me, for I AM coming soon, says the Spirit of Grace.

The spirit of the anti-christ

January 27, 2014

The spirit of the anti-christ. What is the spirit of the anti-Christ? The Lord says the anti-christ spirit is the spirit that denies that Jesus Christ came in the flesh. It's also one that hates to talk about the blood of Jesus. It hates to talk about the resurrected Jesus Christ. And what He did and what He accomplished for us. Oh, yes, there's the unholy trinity now a days. There's the unholy trinity of abortion and homosexuality and also the anti-semitic talk. Because the anti-christ spirit hates the Jews because Jesus Christ was a Jew. So the Lord says I AM going to really upend the anti-christ spirit. I AM going to really deal with it this time. So the Lord says, yes, this is the time and the season when I shall defeat the anti-christ spirit throughout all the land.

The anti-christ spirit is already at work throughout all the earth, among the children of disobedience. Ephesians 2:2. And the Lord says, it shall become evident more and more in the days ahead. You will see the anti-christ spirit all around you like you've never seen it before. You'll see it manifest more in the churches, in the schools, on the news, in social media, in Hollywood, in government, in businesses, in every way. The Holy Spirit says the anti-christ spirit will become emboldened and become bold as the time is short. The enemy will surely show his hand. He won't be cunning about it anymore. He will be forthright. And you will see and clearly know what the anti-christ spirit is more and more every day. So the Lord says you'll be shocked at things that happen in the future. Things that you never dreamed would happen will happen because of the anti-christ spirit, when he shall show his hand. And it shall be ugly. Oh, it shall be ugly. It shall be deceitful. It shall be full of lies. And you'll recognize the anti-christ spirit more and more in the world until finally he shall come upon the scene. But the Lord says be not deceived but walk circumspectly before Me guiding your life by the Word of God. Always refer to the Word of God in every situation. Refer to the Word of God. Know that any spirit that comes against the Blood of Jesus, the Name of Jesus and that He was born of a virgin, in the flesh know that any spirit that would come against these principles has the spirit of the anti-christ. And the Lord says there shall be much talk in churches in the days ahead about inclusion: you must accept this, and this is okay and that's okay. But know all this: It is the spirit of the anti-christ. So the Lord says walk circumspectly before Me (Ephesians 5:15). Redeem the time because of the evil days thereof (Ephesians 5:16). So the Lord says walk upright before Me and you'll not be deceived. For many shall be swept away in the Church in the days ahead. Many shall come under the spell of the anti-christ spirit. But the Lord says you will not because you know My Voice and the voice of a stranger you will not follow, says the Lord thy God. John 10:5.

The Hireling Spirit

January 27, 2014

The thing I AM really starting to deal with, more than ever every day, is the hireling spirit. For the Lord says, oh, yes, the hireling spirit has been in the world, but it has crept into the church more and more every day. So I AM going to deal with the hireling spirit. But first, I AM going to deal with it in the church. For the Lord says, I will not tolerate what they are doing to My Little Ones, to My Sheep, to My Lambs. I will not tolerate it. They only want power and influence and wealth and their name great at the expense of the flock. For that hireling spirit in the Church must go, says the Lord. And I will deal with it also in the government. For that's what we have in the government now. That's why there's a gridlock in the Congress. That's what we have in every branch of the government is the hireling spirit. And I AM going to deal with it. Oh, I'm really going to deal with it in the Military for they have sold this country out. The hireling spirit. Yes, I AM going to deal with it in the school systems, for they're in it for themselves. The unions are in it for themselves. For the Lord says I AM going to totally upset things. Yes, even in the state governments. The hireling spirit even in business. In the banking business. In the Stock Market. I AM going to deal with the hireling spirit in every industry. In every segment of society. For there's nothing but a hireling spirit in the universities. And they're taking advantage of the children. They're taking advantage of the students. They're taking advantage because they want to build a name and a reputation. They want to control. But the Spirit of Grace says unto you today, where sin does abound grace does much more abound. Romans 5:20.

The Lord says, I AM raising up My standard against the enemy for I AM getting rid of the hireling spirit. I AM getting rid of that spirit says the Lord thy God in all this country and in many of the nations around the world where there's a hireling spirit. Yes, I AM going to totally deal with it and the Lord says I AM starting first in the Church, and I AM starting right now. So, you shall see even very shortly, those who have the hireling spirit; especially starting with the Church, they are going to be totally exposed and dealt with. The Lord says I shall not tolerate it any more. The Lord says yes, this is the time and the season where I AM going to expose the evil in this great land, says the Lord.

See also John 10: 11 – 13.

The Masquerade Party

February 19, 2014

For the Lord says, there's a subtle deception; there's a mass deception by the Prince of the power of the air who is satan himself. Yes, it's a subtle deception that if it were, could even deceive some of the very elect of God. Matthew 24:24 But know this: In these last days there shall be many deceptions. There shall be many seducing spirits. There shall be much doctrine of devils and demons. And the Lord says be aware of that which is about to come upon the earth. The Lord says many shall fall into the trap of believing in aliens and in UFOs. But the Lord says this is nothing but the Prince of the power of the air. The flying saucers, the UFOs - this is nothing but a deception and a ruse by the principalities, rulers of darkness, and spiritual wickedness in high places. For the

Word says, he's the Prince of the power of the air. And that's where most of these deceptions take place. People see them in the air. In lights and flying saucers and it's only a mirage. It's only a masquerade. So join the masquerade party if you will. But the Lord says, oh, no! Follow after Me! Follow after Jesus Christ, Who can truly set you free. He's your Savior and not another. For they shall say even these aliens are our savior. Many shall even say they're the ones who created us. And many shall say we have to go and evangelize the aliens. It's a masquerade party that's getting ready to happen. So the Lord says be aware of what's taking place in the earth. For the enemy would try to come in. But the Lord says, I AM going to raise up a standard against the enemy. I AM going to show what he's up to. For even as the lower legions of demons on the earth work with the fallen angels in the heavenly places to bring about this hoax, to bring about such a fraud many people will really believe in flying saucers and they'll really believe in the UFOs. But know ye this: satan is the author of confusion. He's the author of deception. And this is deception on a mass scale. But the Lord says these are days as in the days of Noah. These are days as in the days of Sodom and Gomorrah where there is much evil. And the Lord says, yes, even as in the days of Noah when the DNA of the human race was polluted by the fallen spirits, know this is happening right now. And then there's much talk of trans-humanism. There's much evil that perpetrated for even the principalities and the rulers of darkness are talking to the Hidden Ones.

They're talking about a master race of people that we can develop if we can just tweak the engineering here and the human genes there and slice this and split that. But the Lord says, oh, yes! Be aware! Refuse your invitation to the masquerade party for the Lord says, I shall unmask them. I shall reveal what they're doing and I shall spoil their plans. And the Lord says, yes, man is up to something! They're dreaming of the Tower of Babel once again but I shall stop them in their tracks. For I'm coming soon in all My power and glory says the Spirit of the Lord unto you.

The Greatest Rescue

July 01, 2014

The Lord says soon the greatest rescue, the greatest deliverance that the world has ever seen shall surely be. For the Lord says, the Apple of My Eye, I've got them covered. The Lord says, I shall rescue Israel in the days ahead for the days around the world are drawing to a close. The days are dangerous, but I shall rescue Jewish people from around the world. I shall the rescue the Apple of My Eye. I shall rescue the nation of Israel. Because Israel is entering into a very dangerous time, but I shall be by their side. I shall give them a great rescue and deliverance. And the Lord says at the same time, I AM going to rescue and deliver many Christians around the world. For there are many nations where they're persecuting My children. My Bride. They're all a part of the

Body of Christ. They're all a part of My Bride. And I will not see My Bride slaughtered or persecuted any longer. For the Lord says, I've got many people that you know not of around the world. I've got many people in Iran that are Mine. I've got many in China. Many in Burma. Many even in Vietnam and Cambodia. I have many in the Muslim nations. In the Arab nations. And the Lord says I have many in Africa under oppression. For the Lord says they've been very oppressed. They've been tortured. And I shall deal with them. I shall deal with Castro. I shall deal with Kim in North Korea. I shall deal with that spirit in the Muslim countries that keeps them in bondage. For I have raised up many people but they live in fear and dread. But the Lord says they're going to feel My presence for I AM with them. I will never leave for forsake them. I shall move. I shall move. I shall move in the days ahead. So fear not when you see the great shaking for I shall surely move, says the Lord thy God.

Proverbs 21:1
Psalms 146

Section Two
REVELATIONS

REVELATIONS

End Time Insights

January 02, 2013

The mark of the end time church and move of God will be one of suffering and persecution. This is a different season and time in the earth than the Body of Christ has ever seen. There will without a doubt be physical harm and this type of persecution in some nations and people will lose their lives. (North Korea, Vietnam, China, Muslim Nations, etc). Some will face political persecution (this is happening in the USA now!), but by and large after political persecution, as a group, believers will face economic persecution which will be more severe as we move closer to the tribulation, which I believe we will miss; however, we may go into the first 3 ½ years. (There is an ongoing debate on this matter). I do know this… that soon, religious and maybe secular non profits will lose their tax exempt status. Adjustments shall be made by believers and they shall have great victory, influence, favor as well as great prosperity and find economic success as they move from man's system to God's system. The Body of Christ will thrive financially as they hear God's voice and act but it shall be very painful at first to make the difficult adjustments. Many will wake up and realize they have been mislead for years by ministers with corrupt ways or others who really didn't know God's financial ways but only followed unscriptural concepts of religious traditions. They were simply taught wrong about the way to give financially. I ask you, what is really God's storehouse? Yes, the Lord Jesus and the apostles did accept monetary donations, but never was the money used for the construction of a building, but it was always used for the needs of the people. There are large sums of money raised to build a huge building and to build one's empire. What if some of this money was spent to finance business and to build business wealth that could be used to send the gospel around the world? We see so many who are willing to dedicate their lives to oversee ministry, who work for years with meager support, while there are huge buildings, used only a few times a week or else they are in the daycare business. The Korean and Jewish people have for years put each other in business and we see the power and influence they have. Is it wise to put all this money in large buildings where in other areas the need is great? It is like people who in recent years have become house poor with an oversized house and can't afford furniture. Ministries will be exposed and closed. The last move of God will be by humble, no name people and many miracles will be at the hands of children. God will raise up and teach the Body of Christ simple ways to minister in this new season.

All the above is my humble opinion, but I believe I have the Spirit of the Lord on this matter. Just wait and see what will soon happen to confirm this.

Peace Symbol – Symbol of The antichrist?

June 2011

I have always detested the so called peace symbol. (The broken cross) For some years, you hardly ever saw it. Now in the last few years, you see it everywhere especially on children clothing and to some degree on women's clothing. You see it at every price point. The last time I was in South America, I saw it everywhere.

Is this a worldwide conspiracy? If it is, who ordered it and why?

I came across a book that was all about the Nazi SS elite military units and showed all uniforms and medals and pins they wore. Well along with the lighting bolt pin were about 10 other pins they wore on their uniforms and what they meant. Well there was the peace symbol and the meaning was death. People are walking around wearing a death symbol on their clothing. satan is so subtle. All age and sex groups are being programmed to except this symbol. The anti-christ will come as a man of peace. Will this be his symbol as the swastika was to the Nazis? The swastika was a Hindu symbol that Hitler adopted. In India, the swastika means good luck. I would guess if you dig deep you will find that this symbol goes back to eastern religion also. Several different versions of the swastika were found in Persia and India hundreds of years ago.

New Financial Systems

September 06, 2013

Holy Spirit led organizations, Foundations, and Banks shall be raised up to be financial clearinghouses in the days ahead as wars and financial meltdowns, which have started and shall continue, famine, earthquakes, and economic disruption take place in these United States and around the world. The twin towers of Wall Street and the Federal Reserve Banking System shall fall in a moment's time in New York City, and the Babylonian system will be destroyed. Down will go the tower of Babel in New York City. They seem strong but they are corrupt, a lie that deceived the world and the Lord says, a total fraud just like the IRS, which is a fraud. They were planned and put into place by the same evil men and the whole system along with the World Bank and the IMF. They shall be turned upside down and exposed for all the world to see. I will develop a financial system by and for My remnant people and it will catch Israel by surprise. And, yes, I shall use the Jews to underwrite much of it. I will make the Jewish people jealous of My remnant people! Jewish people will start to realize who they can trust and will start to walk hand in hand with My true believers. The World Reserve Currency - the Dollar - will soon fail; so don't trust in it, the British Pound Sterling, or even the Israeli Shekel. Gold and Silver will even canker and be demanded once again by governments. My people will develop trade and financial systems designed and operated by My Josephs and Daniels. There is a sudden shift and a transformation into the new financial system and, at first, it will be painful with adjustments, but it must come. The world at large shall be amazed and stand in awe. I shall raise up the 5 fold ministry in the market place and as they are led by the Holy Spirit, they shall develop a new economic system. You have no need of a teacher, because you have the Holy Spirit Who is your guide, teacher, and counselor. 1 John 2:27 But especially the babes in Christ will need the 5 fold ministry to come into the unity of the faith. The Apostle shall lead as I give My plans to the Prophets, who work out the details with the Pastors, as the Teachers teach it and the Evangelists spread the news. So there shall be days of awe, days of wonderment, and amazement, as the world sees and understands what a great God I AM and how I made a way for My people. Scores of people will come into the Kingdom of God at this time because of the unity and the love the Body of Christ have one for another.

Wisdom of The Ages

September 18, 2013

The Lord says this is a season that is really different. This is a season when it shall be as it was in ancient times when I shall raise up men and women who will hear My voice and save whole populations, save whole generations from the evil that is coming and from the dark days that are coming. The

Lord says, yes, I have My Joseph Company. I have Daniels. I have the Nehemiahs. I have the Erzas. I have the Esthers. I have the Ruths. I have the Deborahs. I have those that I have set aside for such a time as this. There has always seemed to be a shortage of such people. For there have been one or two or three or four or five; never very many because the time to train somebody and raise them up is very difficult. It takes a long time and most people are really not willing to commit their lives totally to Me in this manner that I might use them for the utmost for My glory. But the Lord says, I AM raising up Daniels and Josephs for the time is coming. Yes, the time is coming. There will have to be Daniels and Josephs and Esthers and Ruths. For the time is coming. The time is coming when the Body of Christ won't know what to do. The world will be in disarray and many people will disappear from the face of the earth, if I didn't raise up those who would walk in My wisdom. So the Lord says in the days ahead, it is going to become evident who those around you are that are the Daniels and the Josephs and the Deborahs. For the Lord says, I AM going to raise them up. I AM going to raise up modern day Priscillas and Acquillas that worked with Paul in tent making. For the Lord says, I AM raising up a people in the market place. I AM raising up people in governments. I AM raising up people in the banking systems. I AM raising up people that will have the mind of Christ. That will have My mind and can direct and give instruction about what to do in the days ahead. For there is a time of preparation that must be. A time to prepare for the unexpected. A time to prepare for the evil that is coming. I AM going to give a short time so My people can prepare, but My people don't know that suddenly evil will overwhelm them. Suddenly they will be shocked at events that shall overtake them in the earth. The Lord says I AM raising up very quietly the Zerubbabels. I AM raising up very quietly those that will stand on the wall in such a time as this. And, yes, most of them are intercessors. Most of them wait before Me. They wait before Me in quietness and they hear My voice. Most of them even seem insignificant and the world at large would never recognize them much less the religious. But the Lord says, I've got My remnant people. I've got My people that are the vanguard and they shall go out in the days ahead. And you will be surprised at one who seems weak but he'll be bold in the days ahead. He'll be a Joseph. He'll be a Daniel. She'll be a Deborah. She'll be an Esther. I will raise him up in this time. So the Lord says, don't fear. Don't fear. I've got things covered in the days ahead. You'll know who they are. Soon it will become evident who they are for they shall have the wisdom, the wisdom that is needed in the coming days. For the days are dark indeed, but in the midst of famine and destruction, I will have a people, I will have a remnant people. I will have a people that will lead out. I will have those that have been through the test. Have been through the trials. Have been through the fires even as Joseph was. Even as Daniel was. For I shall raise up those in the governments. I shall raise up those who will know how to make sure provision. Who will know how to set up a financial system in the days ahead. For I shall supernaturally impart unto them My wisdom because they know My voice and the voice of a stranger they will not follow. John 10:5 The Lord says you will get to know them and you can trust them, says the Spirit of the Lord for they are of Me. I will give you a sign and a way to know who they are. And the Lord says, yes, they will have My wisdom. The wisdom of the ages I shall impart unto them, says the Lord thy God.

Liar Liar

September 19, 2013

The Lord would say liar, liar pants on fire. New lies told for the same old lies in the days ahead. Lies. Lies. Lies. One branch of the government will lie to the next branch of the government. The Congress shall lie to the Executive Branch. The Executive Branch shall lie to the Congress. Democrats shall lie to Republicans. Republicans shall lie to each other. Democrats shall lie to each other. The Judicial Branch shall lie to everyone. She said. He said. They said. There shall be much blame in the days ahead. All around the world there shall be great confusion in all the governments of all the major countries of the world, as one lie is told to another lie. Everything shall seem to unravel. Yes, there shall be collapses of governments. There shall be collapses of the economy. Yes, you shall see the huge Transnational Corporations - many came out of America - you shall see them decline and many shall even go bankrupt in the days ahead.

And the Lord says things shall be very different in the days ahead. Even the hidden ones, those that have plotted for many years, shall be totally exposed; for they have moved quicker than they should. They have made many bad decisions. And yes, it shall bring down, as it were, the whole house of cards. It shall bring down the roof on top of them, says the Lord thy God. For they have miscalculated and they have brought ruin when they didn't really want to bring such a ruin. They only wanted to bring a little disaster here and a little disaster there but they have brought down the roof on top of their heads. And truly the Lord says, I shall unravel many things in the days ahead. For, yes, the Lord says, I shall unravel the whole situation at the Federal Reserve Banking System. Keep your eyes on what's going on there, for I AM going to turn it upside down. Keep your eyes on the IRS, for I AM going to turn it upside down. For both of these are part of the Communist Manifesto that was talked about and written about. For the Lord says, I AM going to expose it. I AM going to expose dozens and dozens of Communists in the Government, says the Lord thy God. Those that are Marxist. Those that are anti-American, but they say they really are Americans. I AM going to expose those in politics on both sides in the United States; in both parties, where the Communists have embedded themselves. The Marxists have embedded themselves. The Lord says, I AM going to bring down that which the enemy has brought into this country. I AM going to totally undo the enemy's plans in the days ahead. For the Lord says, there is a great failure of the dollar. There's a great failure of this country. There's a great failure of this government and it could even collapse. And the Lord says for days at a time there's going to be confusion. And even the military, which should be stable, shall be upside down. And the Lord says, in all this, many malls shall close. Many big chains of restaurants shall close. And the Lord says, yes, there shall be shortages. There shall be distribution problems. The Lord says the economy in the future is going to be very different than it is today. For it shall go back more to Mom and Pop stores. It shall go back to many things being locally produced and made. For the Lord says, I AM going to shrink the economy. I AM going to even stop what the enemy has planned. The Lord says in this country, your life around the world shall change drastically in the days ahead. And the Lord says, I AM taking down the systems of man and I AM going to put in My systems. I AM going to bring the Daniels and Josephs to the forefront. And the Lord says, keep your eyes posted on world events. Keep your eyes on the election that's coming soon in Germany. Keep your eyes on Bavaria, Germany. Keep your eyes on what shall happen in Germany for great change shall soon come to Germany. For it shall be a dangerous country in the days ahead. But keep your eyes on Germany.

Keep your eyes on the falling and fallout of the International Global Companies. Keep your eyes on Wall Street for it shall totally collapse. The Lord says trust not in man or mammon, but trust in Me. Trust not in riches or gold, but trust in Me. For I AM going to bring about a new order even as the hidden ones want to bring about the New World Order, I AM going to bring about My order in this time. I AM going to raise up My people to be victorious in this time. So the Lord says, fear not, for all this must happen. For the great shaking has started and the great shaking shall continue. And people shall be in dread and fear as they awake every day, because of the uncertainties. Because there shall not be anything left that is normal - seemingly normal - that you know is normal anymore. For institutions shall collapse. The Lord says I AM going to bring about My plan in the earth. And the Lord says, in the middle of war - because war is coming and a greater war is coming and destruction, fires, earthquakes, pestilence, disease such as the world has never known shall be released - but the Lord says, in the middle of what is happening, in the middle of all the shaking that shall come upon the earth, I AM going to move by My Spirit. And you think, how can it be? How can you send out missionaries to other nations in confusion? But the Lord says I AM going to upright the apple cart and I AM going to put My new apples into the apple cart, says the Lord thy God. And the Lord says don't be dismayed. I AM going to upright the apple cart and put new apples in and I AM going to cause a whole new order to come into existence for My people shall rise up with a strong voice.

And they shall say and they shall do what I tell them to do and they shall walk in boldness and great courage and the God kind of faith. For the Lord says I AM totally undoing the wickedness. I AM totally going to undo what the enemy has done.

So lies, lies, lies. In the days ahead, Wall Street shall be telling lies that all is okay. The Federal Reserve Banking System shall be telling lies that all is okay. The International Monetary Fund. The World Bank. They all shall be telling lies to the public and then they'll tell lies to each other. The truth will not be found in them. And even the hidden ones in Northern Europe, they'll be telling lies to each other. Great deception is coming on the earth. A lying spirit. But the Lord says the Father of all Lies shall be revealed for who he truly is. For I AM raising up a generation that will speak the truth in love. I AM raising up a generation that shall speak about the truth of the gospel of Jesus Christ and how it shall set the captive free. The Lord says, I shall set many captives free in the days ahead for the gospel shall be the only thing that shall be stable in the world. For the gospel of Jesus Christ shall be the only thing that shall bring stability to the world. So the Holy Spirit will lead and guide you in the days ahead and He will tell you to turn to the right and turn to the left. And you must listen to the voice of the Spirit that you won't be lost or faint or falter in the days ahead. Listen to the voice of the Holy Spirit. For you know the voice of your Father. You know the voice of Jesus. I shall raise up many to be a voice crying in the wilderness. So prepare ye the way for the coming of the Lord is soon.

"Issachar Generation"

September 09, 2013

This is not a prophecy such as the Lord said, but nevertheless, in the Spirit of prophecy. It is musing and meditative that I received after being with the Lord. I see that I am a man of unclean lips and I live among a people of unclean lips, (Isaiah 6:5) but verse 7, my lips and mouth have been touched and verse 8, the Lord said He would send me and I said "Here am I, send me." Verse 9 Go and tell the people who are ever hearing but never understanding and who see, but don't perceive or understand the times and seasons and that the "Time of the Gentiles" is coming to an end and the "Day of the Lord" is close at hand! Verse 10 Their eyes are closed and their ears dull and hearts are calloused. Soon the cities will lie in ruins and fields ravaged, but in this God is still God, and because of prayers of the saints and our ancestors who looked to God, I did hear God say "America will be America again," to some degree. Some in the future will even try to compare it to the late 40s, 50s, and 60s.

Change is coming in all the world. Many things will become more simple but yet dangerous, like it was in the Cold War, but more so. Many parts of the country will repent and God will move, but there will be pockets that will resist God!

There is, however, a move of God coming in the schools, the market place, the government, and the military. No one will be able to stop it around the world. Much evil will be exposed and these United States will move back towards the idea of the Founding Fathers. God is saying He is going to slow everything down so people will look to Him and have time for Him to move in their lives. The Father is saying even My people have become too busy being busy! The Bible does say in the End Times, travel and knowledge will increase and it has. Travel will be more difficult in some places in the days ahead and God is telling me He is slowing down the technology advances and people will question... can they totally trust and depend 100% on computers? We have already seen some problems in the stock market, etc. Also the problems with hackers will become worse with each passing day. There are coming shortages and labor and distribution problems. Many large malls and chain restaurants and transnational corporations will suffer great losses and decline. Work hours and retail business hours will be shortened for several reasons. Many large commercial centers around the world shall suffer loss and destruction, including New York City. James 5: 1-8.

There shall be a slowdown of technology because the Holy Spirit said it has to slow down or the anti-christ would come on the stage before it is his time. Also, if knowledge increases further, it will be like a modern day Tower of Babel and all will speak the same language and nothing will be able to stop mankind from doing what he wants even living for hundreds of years. We are in the time of great wars (I Thessalonians 5:4) and the day of scoffers. (II Peter 3:3).

We will need to separate ourselves from the world system and their ways. We need to store up, I heard God say, for five years, but not be hoarders Obadiah 1:15. The Holy Spirit says, He is raising up a remnant people who have an understanding of the times and seasons and know what Israel and the Church should do. I Chronicles 12:32 A people who do know their God and shall be strong and do exploits. Daniel 11:33 They shall understand and instruct many even when it shall be difficult. Time will be shortened or even the elect will be deceived and the earth destroyed. Soon, new weapons will be in place 100 times worse than nuclear weapons. So work for Him for time is running out. It is a race against time. The tipping point is almost here.

The Old and The New

October 16, 2013

Oh, it shall seem strange in the days ahead, says the Lord thy God for there shall be a mixture of the old and new. As in some situations and in some times things, will go back to the old technology and the old way of doing things. For some things, it shall be like in the 40s, 50s, and 60s and things will change so the new technology will not be reliable. The Lord says, it is a different season. It is a different time. It shall be strange. Some things shall be so modern and yet some things shall be so old. And some things that seem so out of date shall be new again. For the Lord says it shall be a mixed bag. For the Lord says some of the newer things shall become unreliable all of a sudden. And some people will look backwards instead of forward. And the Lord says even – oh, yes, I shall no longer open up the heavens for more space exploration says the Lord thy God. For the Lord says, the secret things belong unto the Lord. Deuteronomy 29:29 And some things in the heavenlies are secrets and they belong unto Me. For if men went there, it would create so many problems and it would even create a Tower of Babel effect. And the knowledge would be so increased. But the Lord says, I AM going to slow down the knowledge. I AM going to slow down the technology. But the Lord says man would seem to take over as it were in the Tower of Babel days if I didn't stop him and bring confusion into the camps of the peoples of the earth. For the Lord says oh, yes, I AM behind many of the shakings which you shall see in the days ahead in the technology market. For things shall be very different. And the Lord says even as in the 30s, 40s, 50s and 60s when the Communists almost took over the United States, the Lord says, it's the same way again. The Communists are on the verge of taking over the United States again. But the Lord says, even as events stopped it back then, and slowed it down, this time I shall totally undo them. I shall totally expose them and depose them. And the Lord says, even you shall be shocked and surprised in the days ahead. Some people that you would never have dreamed are hidden Communists shall come out that they are Communists. And the Lord says, some that you would think would be Liberals and that they would be Communists are not Communists but are horrified by the prospects of it. And the Lord says, oh, yes, it shall be the old and the new in the days ahead. For the Lord says, things are different now than they have ever been. For, yes, you have entered into the new season that I have told you about. And even as you go into 2014, you shall see things shall be so strange and things shall be so unique. Things shall be so dangerous. And the Lord says, yes, there shall be many upsets of governments in the days ahead; financial markets collapsing, governments collapsing, lies told everywhere, new lies for old lies. The old lies told once again. People shall believe a lie. But the Lord says, yes, even those that have believed a lie, many shall have their eyes opened in the days ahead. For this is a time in the earth when I shall bring enlightment. I shall bring enlightment to many and many shall start to see where they have gone wrong in the days ahead. For the days ahead shall be many days of confusion. Many days of confusion. But the Lord says in the midst of confusion, in the midst of war which is soon coming, I shall move, says the Lord thy God. Yes, didn't I say that I would upset the apple cart and that they would re-gather the apples? For the Lord says, in many situations I AM going to turn that apple cart back upright and put new, fresh apples in it. I AM going to bring many people in which are of Me, into the government, into the military, and into important places in the government, in finances, and in Hollywood. I have a Kingdom people that I have saved for such a time as this. And I AM going to have My people put in important places. I will have the Daniels, the Josephs, the Elijahs, the Ezras, the Nehemiahs, and the Zerubbabels. I shall bring them forth in this hour. They're going to walk in boldness and in power. For there shall be some things of old. There shall be some things of new. It shall be a mixture, says the Lord thy God. But know that in days of confusion when it seems so strange, I AM in the midst of all the change. I AM in the midst of the upsets that you shall see. And you shall see how I shall use many upsets, many situations that are turned upside down, you shall see how I shall use them for My glory, says the Lord thy God.

A Flame of Fire

October 17, 2013

This is what the Lord revealed to me last night. It's a revelation or end time insight through a prophecy. We will be flames of fire for God in the days ahead. Hebrews 1:7 a constant Holy Spirit fire, a burning holy inward flame. Just like Jesus was in the world. We have to have a living growing faith so the power and might can flow through us it will energize us. We will be God's energizer bunnies. A flame for our God. We will walk as kings in His resurrection power. Acts 1:8 "You shall receive power when the Holy Spirit is come on you" 1 John 4:4 the greater power is within you. It's greater than the power that is within the world. So let God be a flame of fire for you. And the Lord is telling me that even in the days ahead, when He brings up the Ezras, the Nehemiahs, the Zerubabbels, the Joshuas the Calebs and even when He brings in the spirit of Elijah and the spirit of Moses. The Lord is saying these people who He is going to be raising up are going to be like these men. And like Deborah and like Ruth and like Esther. These men and women shall be bold. They shall be flames of fire. And the Lord says, I AM going to rise up this company of remnant believers. I will bring them before governments. I will bring them before militaries I will bring them before royalty. I will bring them before rulers in this world and authorities. And the Lord says, they shall be flames of fire for Me.

And the Lord says, they will go in before them, even as Moses went in before Pharaoh. And they will say, this is what you're going to do! This is the way it's going to be! In the Name of Jesus, this is what you will do. This is what you won't do! And they shall be bold. And if they are threatened, the Lord says, there'll be angels that surround them. Furthermore, if they are touched, the Lord says, a flash of electricity or like a stun gun or like a flash of fire shall flow out of their hands as they point their hands in their direction. And everybody shall fall down under the power of God with this electrical charge which is the Holy Spirit. Some will even be blinded for a day or so. And the Lord says My people are going to in this kind of power. And the Lord says, it's not for retaliation. It's not as they will. And it's not for their financial purpose. Because people would even say, I want to buy that power from you. But the Lord says, this is the power of God. These are signs and wonders and miracles. And this shall be a sign to those authorities that God is in their midst. This shall be a sign of the authority that these people walk in. The Lord says, yes, they shall use this power for My glory, but it's not their own power. It's a power of the Holy Spirit. It shall disarm these people. It shall be a sign and a wonder. Even as Moses had signs and wonders and miracles in this midst. So it shall be like an electric stun gun that will go out as they point their hand out. It shall be like a flame of fire that will go out and touch these people and they will be afraid of these people's faces. They shall be afraid and in fear of what manner of man is this? And they shall say, you even walk as gods. And that person shall say, no, this is the power of the Holy Spirit. This is the power of Jesus Christ. Repent now, while you have the chance!

For the Lord says in the days ahead, it will be very different. The Body of Christ shall walk in the power and the authority and the resurrection power of Jesus Christ. And signs and wonders shall truly follow them. In the Name of Jesus, they will say do this. Do that. I'm walking and I'm moving because in Him you live and move and have your being. Acts 17:28 for the Lord says it shall be different in the days ahead. It shall be a power and an authority that the Body of Christ has not walked in before. It shall be the same kind of authority that Jesus walked in. For the Lord says greater works shall you do. So you shall hear about and know about these great works. And some of you will be the ones who do these greater works in the days ahead, says the Lord your God.

End Time Events

October 17, 2013

The Lord says there is coming great war. There is coming great destruction. But, yes, after that shall come a great spiritual awakening which shall start in Philadelphia and go up and down the East Coast and move around the world. It shall be a move of God that shall really shake the earth. It shall shake the country. It shall shake the nations. For the Lord says there shall be such a flow of My Holy Spirit that whole countries shall come to Me in a matter of weeks or months. The Lord says I shall move across the face of the earth. Is My hand shortened that I cannot save and deliver? (Isaiah 59:1). Oh, yes, I shall totally transform this country once again and the universities. And the government. And the military. And the schools. I shall move in this country. I shall do a quick work. And then soon after that I shall come. Because the Lord says, even after this great move of the Holy Spirit. You shall slowly see things start to deteriorate again, as people start to forget about Me. As Christians become cold and their love for Me will wax cold. (Mathew 24:12) and the Lord says there shall be a great falling away from Me. And because of that I will come quickly. (Matthew 24:22) the Lord says, then a great war. A great move of God. And then the start of a great falling away. So I will come quickly. So redeem the time because of the evil days thereof. Ephesians 5:16 Behold I will not tarry. Behold I AM coming quicker, even that you can imagine. Yes, I AM coming quickly.

And the Lord says in this great move of God shall be signs, and wonders, and miracles such as you have never seen or even could imagine. Even the small children shall operate in signs and wonders and miracles. The Lord says truly this is the time when I shall move with My Holy Spirit's power without measure in all the earth. So look for Me. Look for the soon coming King, coming in all His glory and power. The Lord says, be faithful unto Me, My Little Ones.

Section Three
DREAMS

DREAMS

In The Classroom Situation With Hitler

One night in 80s, I had a dream that took place sometime in the late 50s or early 60s, judging by the furniture. I was in a classroom (viewing it from the ceiling). The student's desks were oak with a hole for the inkwell, and the teacher's desk was a large, oak library table.

Looking down from the ceiling, I was able to see the back and top of the teacher's head. There were about 15 students-all boys about 10 to 12 years of age. Each one had three adult tutors sitting around him. Looking closer, I was amazed that everyone was dressed in well-tailored black Nazi SS uniforms. I began to move to the back of the classroom while still above at the ceiling. In shock, I noticed the teacher had grey hair and a full mustache. His face was the face of Hitler. He looked to be about 65-70 years old and bore an evil grin. He had just asked a question, and one of the boys had the answer but was too shy to reply right away. His tutor tapped him on the shoulder prompting him to speak. He had the right answer. The man who resembled Hitler smiled happily and said, good work.

Within two weeks, I received two research books about Hitler and both claimed he had escaped-one said to South America on a submarine. The books mentioned a secret group called Odessa, which hid high Nazi officers.

What do you think? Interesting. Shortly after this dream, a movie came out called *The Boys from Brazil* which was a story about Hitler being cloned.

A Series of Dreams

Gorbachev

Russian leader Mikhail Gorbachev was on television but the sound was muted, so all I could do was watch him speaking. Suddenly, the red birthmark on his head jumped out and these words came to me: You can never trust him…he is a master deceiver. (As of 2011, he has a foundation in California that advocates a "green" socialism).

Middle East…

Later that night, I dreamed I was in the Middle East. A well-dressed Arab in western clothing was on television with a map behind him. He had a pointer in his hand. Again, the sound was muted, so I couldn't hear his words but these words came to me: There will soon be a war in the Middle East. Soon after this was the first war in Iraq.

God Is Speaking

Deception in the church....

One night, I had a dream that I was standing in the back of a church that was a metal building. It was very crowded with about 800 people inside. While we were in praise and worship, there erupted a loud noise and someone announced that Jesus' brother was here. I decided I'd check it out when I saw four men carrying a man up front in a chair with poles running through-a type of sedan chair indigenous to India or China in ancient times. The man didn't look Jewish to me, more like Eastern Indian, like a guru. I began to jump up and down, shouting to everyone that they are being deceived, while they, in turn, began to shout back at me.

The next night, I came home and while sitting at my desk turned on public television. They said to stay tuned because in 15 minutes an Englishman will be talking about "The Christ" who, according to him, will be revealed to the world. He said this is the same "lord" that ran full-page ads in the 70s saying, "The Christ" will soon be revealed. This older gentleman, Benjamin Crème, explained his revelation (ESP), etc. and said that soon the stock market will crash in Japan, Europe, and the USA. This was January of 1990, and he had said it would happen by March. Well, the stock market in Japan did start to fall and I came against it in prayer that it would stop and not continue to fall. They showed a picture of this guy on television and it was the same man I had seen in the dream in the church the night before—an Indian they called "Lord Maitreya"!

Germany...

In 1990, I kept having dreams that Germany is going to rise again and that it will be a very dangerous place for Jews and Christians. That spirit behind Hitler is still there. I believe we will go back into isolation and have similar conditions to those before WWII. Jesus had 12 disciples and Hitler appointed 12 Field Marshalls. In several dreams, the Lord says that Germany is a country to watch—a very dangerous country. Could the anti-christ come out of Germany? Many say the Middle East, but I believe it will be from Europe—the old Roman Empire. I know it will happen.

Russia, early Sunday morning, 1990...

The USA had a military camp or post with Russia. In the dream, I saw the Russian flag flying and the USA flag flying next to the flags of three or four smaller countries. The Russians told the other smaller countries that the USA doesn't have to pay for their share of the base because they are neutral. (Then my alarm clock went off.) Several hours later, I saw the headlines in the newspaper: "Pentagon makes even deeper military cuts." Could we be in for a time of isolation again as before WWII?

Martial Law Washington D.C.

During the second term of Bill Clinton, I had a dream that Washington was under martial law with U.N. troops on every street corner. The foreign troops wore the uniforms of their countries along with U.N. sky blue berets. The "peacekeepers" were Russian, Dutch, German, Belgian and the Marines and they were the only ones on the very quiet and otherwise empty streets. Suddenly, a Marine colonel and about 300 other men and officers showed up at the old marine barracks, just southeast of the Capitol off Pennsylvania Avenue. They had several army trucks full of heavy machine guns and small arms from Ft. Myers in Arlington, VA. There are about 2,000 unarmed Marines and the colonel said to get ready to go. We are going to take our country back. We're going to disarm the U.N. troops and arrest the President and others for treason

As they start up Pennsylvania Avenue, they head into an African American area and a number of black men start to pour out of their homes with U.S. Marine flags and caps, saying that they want to help. The colonel said, yes, take your neighborhoods back, and disarm the foreign troops, while also instructing them to get rid of the terrible U.N. berets! As the Marines move up Pennsylvania Avenue, they see troops on every street corner—always three on each block (a U.S. Marine and two others, either Dutch, German, Belgian or Russian). They put up no resistance. The surprise was that quite a few of the Russian troops said that they have always loved the USA and admired our freedom and liberty. They said they wanted to help the Americans take back their country and became citizens. The colonel said, yes, we will help you, just disarm the other U.N. troops and you and the Marines watch them. So they arrive at the White House with no problems. The Marine colonel said we are going to arrest a lot of people for treason and restore their country to a constitutional republic. All over Washington, hundreds were being arrested. Also, in N.Y.C., arrests were underway at that very hour, and Henry Kissinger was being arrested for treason.

So the colonel and officers along with about 100 men start walking up the sidewalk next to the White House near the black wrought iron fence. Out on the White House lawn was the President with about 12 secret service men carrying short machine guns from Israel. The head of his detail said to the Marines, "Stop! What is your intent?" The colonel told them that we'd come to arrest the President for treason. The Secret Service said, "Don't come any closer. We will protect him and fire on you." The colonel said, "Look, we have hundreds of Marines here. We will take him and you will die for nothing. We are fellow Americans and you know he is full of treason." So the agent talked for a few minutes and said, "Yes, we will put our weapons down and you can have the traitor. Arrest him." In the dream, I could only see the President at a distance; he looked to be in his 60s with white hair, standing six feet tall. Who does that describe? Bill Clinton, Joe Biden and Newt Gingrich.

The Stage - Dream – Washington, D.C., 1996

Words in the dream – "Blow the trumpet in Zion!" "Sound the Alarm!" "War! War!"

The stage is being set. The curtain is drawn. Behind the curtain, the stagehands are busy getting the stage set for the play. I could hear them moving things around as they worked to get ready. The color of the curtain is the same blue as in the Israeli flag. Across the curtain in large gold letters is the word, "Israel." I heard the Spirit of God saying, woe unto those who would come against Israel. Woe to those who deal in treachery or trickery. Those who deal in a crafty way. Israel is the apple of God's eye. We are in the latter years!

Dream Of Trip To Bank in Switzerland 2000

In this dream, I was awakened by an angel who wanted me to hurry and get dressed, specifically wanting me to put on my sport coat-the one with lots of pockets. Then we were immediately transported to a bank in Switzerland. Standing in front of a huge vault, the angel touched the doors and they opened, revealing banded piles of American hundred dollar bills. He told me to take them and put them in my coat pockets. In a second visit, the angel told me the same thing, but there were gold bars to collect this time. Another visit yielded more hundred dollar bills. Each time, the angel said to talk no more or less that what I tell you.

A View Of The World

April 2010

I have had several dreams where Jesus the Son, or an angel would visit me. But for the first time, God the Father came to me. (It was a whole different feeling.) God, himself, took me to the highest mountain on earth. The view was like traveling in an airplane at night and viewing the lights below. God was about 12 feet behind me and three feet to the left. I could have spied Him out of the corner of my left eye, but I didn't dare look. His voice was loud and full of authority. He said, I am going to show you some things to come.

Before God could tell me anything, behind Him and to His left, satan came up the mountains. Mostly, just an outline of some man-like creature with short arms and legs. I could hear God back-hand him and said, "Get out of here. It's not yet your time to come to the earth and do you most wicked deeds."

Then God began to show me different parts of the earth. First, He showed me the brightly lit UK, and then he said that, once again, the lights would shine in the USA, UK, Canada, Australia and New Zealand, and they would take the gospel to world. Then He showed me Europe. There were only a few dim lights shining there. He said, "Look, I gave them a great church buildings, culture, arts, social advancements, and they turned their back on me." Then a huge bright light came up from Bern, Switzerland and I was suddenly transported there. I met a couple—he looked to be in his 50s with salt and pepper hair and a mustache, and she had light, shoulder-length hair. He smiled and said hello before I was transported again in a flash to the top of the mountain with God.

Then God showed me Asia, and there we so many bright lights shining up from the earth that I was almost blinded. He took me to China, India, Indonesia, the Philippines and smaller nations. All were very bright, except for Japan. Finally, He said, "Nations shall come to me in a short period of time…some in just a matter of months. This is the time when I will move into a great harvest in the earth."

Economic Crisis Europe

January 2011,

For some weeks now, I've started to feel an urgent call to pray about the economic situations. I wasn't sure if something further was going to happen to the USA or Europe. Then I read about the problems in Ireland, Portugal, Spain, etc. About this time, my wife, Ana Ruth, had a dream. She was in a city with tall, shiny silver buildings; man was standing behind a building about 50 stories tall that looked like dull pewter. He then fell forward right on his face.

I knew what it was. The E.U. and the Euro will fall. It reminded me of a series of dreams I had of Germany about 15 years ago and how it would rise to power again, and France would be its proxy. In one dream, I heard the words, Germany, Germany, Germany…much evil will come out of German, once again. Tell the Jews to leave all of Europe, especially Germany. In the future, it will not be a safe place for Christians or Jews.

In a separate dream, I heard these words three times, victory over the German Bank.

Dreams Of Hometown And War…

July 2011

On a Friday night, I had a dream of my hometown of 25,000 in northwest Tennessee. Suddenly, I arrived there; however, I don't remember driving in—just put there. I was in shock to see the old red brick courthouse in the downtown square had been burned to the ground with smoke rising from the building. The main street, Court Street, runs straight to the old family home about one mile east. There was a man in his

30s standing in the middle of the street running straight to the old family home. He looks to be in shock. As I stared at the fires, I told him that I wanted to go and see the condition of the old home. He said I could go but that he's sure it was gone. He said things were terrible, and the farther up the street, the worse it would get. There were no other people around, and I turned to leave.

On a Saturday night, I had a dream that I am on the Mexico-USA border where there is a border war. There's been an invasion and we were being pushed farther back on our side of the border. One the south side, I saw a huge number of people coming in, but I couldn't see their faces or uniforms—just heavy machine guns and small arms fire. We were outnumbered, and I saw no US military, except for some small National Guard units. We were being pushed back more each hour. Then all across the West, Southwest, and Midwest, I saw men loading their cars and trucks with guns, ammo, water, food, dogs, and thousands were heading for the border. They started to gain the upper hand, pushing them back. It was a fierce battle.

Washington's Vision

July 2011

On a Sunday night, I was reading a newspaper book review about a new book on George Washington. They title was something like, "The Seeds of Revolution – George Washington." It was about his training by the British and the raising up of a Virginia army to go north and fight in the French and Indian War. The French were killing all of the British and American officers, and the professional British turned tail, panicked and ran. The army from Virginia was defeated. Washington had three bullets go into his clothes and two horses were shot out from under him. He knew then that the British could be defeated and that God was with him because he was not killed. He knew he and America had a destiny. I then remembered the angels who visited him at Valley Forge that told him of three great perils the new country would face. The angel had said, "Now, was the first...the second would be brother against brother, and the worst would be the third-you would be invaded all across the country...towns and villages would be set on fire." All hope would seem lost, but the people would take heart and push the enemy back into the sea and across the border. One of the angels had a crown on his head that read, "Union"; he held a sword in his hand and said even if the whole world were against you, the USA would win.

*The reason I'm sharing Washington's vision is because it supports some of my own visions and dreams.

Rebirth Of The Holy Roman Empire

February 24, 2013

Early one Sunday morning, I dreamed there were ancient buried statues and monuments of stone or granite that appeared to be leaders of governments, or military figures with armor, similar to a Greek or Roman soldier. Suddenly, they were pushed out of the ground like a tulip or buttercup would come up in the spring (about six to eight figures). As they came up, they were caked with dirt until the rain cleaned them. (While the dirt is being cleaned off, could this imply a transition time before the renewed Holy Roman Empire comes back to life?) It's puzzling. Then the Holy Spirit began to speak to me in a clear voice: Monumental days are just ahead which will have a long and lasting impact on the earth. Massive change is coming to peoples' lives, and political, military and governmental systems will be swept away. I heard these words: "Beware of the Ides of March."

The Holy Spirit was very clear in saying that the times and seasons of the earth were about to change. A time we can't even imagine. Europe, in particular, will become a dangerous place for Christians and Jews…especially, German Jews. They need to leave that place right away! The selection of the new Pope will start the most evil time in the history of mankind! This time will be the rebirth or resurrection of the old Holy Roman Empire. It will be everything but holy! It will be the most despicable time there ever has been for Christians and Jews. Utter contempt for the believers! Walls shall be broken down between Jews and Christians as they rush to embrace and protect each other. Such a time of tyranny and despotism, the mind can hardly fathom because it shall be so evil. The worst places shall be within the borders of the Old Roman

Empire.

But the world at large shall walk in dread and fear at the power that My remnant people shall have at their disposal as they walk upon the earth in My manifest glory that shall protect them as they do exploits in My name. This is a time I will make My name great in the earth, and they shall be afraid of the boldness of My Holy Spirit-directed people as the move in the earth. Yes, destruction from war and earthquakes is coming, but also a great spirited move that shall usher millions in the Kingdom of God. Your old enemy, satan, will oppose it, but "Greater is He who is in you than he who is in the world" (1 John 4:4). Nothing on this earth or under the earth or in the air shall be able to stop the manifestation of the sons and daughters of God. This is what renowned men of ancient days longed to see, but My precious ones shall be caught up in it. Yes, it shall be a quick work, and then I will come in all My glory and power for all the world to see! Prepare you the way of the Lord! "The day of the Lord is at hand!" (Joel 2:1.)

Special Note of Interest

Buying an Auto… Caution!

In the early 90s, I was speaking in a church in Washington, D.C., and the Lord told me to tell the people to pray before they purchased an SUV—particularly, the Ford Explorer. (Well, several people were a little unhappy with me!) About two years later, there was a problem with the Explorer rolling over as well as a problem with a certain brand of tires. Now for about a year, the Lord has been telling me to tell people to really pray before they purchase any new autos from Europe—especially, German autos. Now, don't be angry with me! I love German cars but one of the big problems the Lord showed me would be extra spare parts for these autos and the means to keep them serviced and running. I'm not telling you NOT to buy one; just pray and make sure you have the leading of the Holy Spirit. Really, you should get the mind of the Lord on all your large purchases!

The Hidden World Rulers

June 07, 2013

I had the same dream on Friday and Saturday nights (June 7th and 8th) in 2013. The Holy Spirit had shared with us in the prayer room that a small group of people who live high in the mountains of Switzerland, Liechtenstein, Luxembourg, and to a lesser degree, Austria (close to where the money is), control the rulers of the world and give them their general goals and marching orders. If they don't carry out these orders, they face ruin or even in some cases, death. God is going to expose and depose these people! In these last days of this age, they will turn on each other as events unfold in the earth. The anti-christ is about to come forth and he will not share power with anyone. In this dream, God showed me how Lucifer gives instructions to his puppets.

I saw a man and woman in their late 40s to early 50s in

leather chairs in a well-appointed, yet simple room with walnut paneled walls. Both were from northern Europe. Their clothes were plain classic styles in solid colors and well-tailored. He was wearing a navy cashmere blazer with grey flannel trousers and a blue shirt. He had an empty glass in his hand and seemed to be in a dazed stupor. In her hand was also a small glass with a short stem and small base. She kept whirling the contents around as though it were wine. It reminded me of a whirling tornado with the base of the glass representing the earth. The contents of the glass looked like sparkling glacier water laced with something lethal. Liquid opium? It was a secret mixture that Lucifer had revealed to them to open their minds and spirits to receive his instructions from fallen spirits for a one world government. This involved his timetable and the next steps to take. He knows his time is short! (Psalm 75 – Living Bible and amplified. Isaiah 51:16, 17, 22, 23 and Daniel 2:20-23.)

Section Four
VISIONS

VISIONS

Vision Of Moon And Islam

April 2006.

I was living in Oklahoma City. Usually, before I went to bed (about midnight), I would walk out onto the patio and just pray and say a final goodnight to the Lord, taking a look at all of the stars and just feel in awe of God's greatness. This particular night, the moon was a quarter moon and had some cloud coverage, and the sky was a different color than usual—a blue grey color, almost a gun metal blue. Everything in the sky had this color. While I viewed the moon, a larger moon to the right of the quarter moon took over the smaller one. I closed my eyes and reopened them to see that it still looked the same. It was puzzling as to the meaning

Later, in June, I went to Bogota, Columbia where I conducted my final service. We had a wonderful anointed time in the Lord and felt a great rush of His Holy Spirit. About 3:30 AM, the Lord woke me up and I then realized the meaning of the vision: There are two major divisions of Islam—Sunni and Shiite—and the one shall overtake the other, and there shall be a great struggle and much bloodshed. The average Muslim on the street shall have his eyes open and realize this is no religion of peace but only more and more bloodshed. Then their eyes will begin to open to Jesus Christ.

Weapons Technology
Secrets Revealed To My Remnant People!

November 2012

I kept having dreams and visions that showed me a new surge in technology that will rapidly change how business is conducted. The more important things revealed to me concern Israel and their relations with the USA.

Many nations see the USA as the one who protects Israel, much like a big brother. But this is changing. Many believe that the CIA, FBI, etc. have stopped violent attacks against us, but it is Israel who has given us information that has prevented thousands of acts of terror. The US Government has requested that it not be revealed who gave us the information. It would not be prudent for Israel to divulge this information because they want to remain stealth and not compromise their sources.

Nuclear weapons will soon be used, but shortly after that, they will become obsolete. There is a weapon ready that is 100 times more powerful than nuclear weapons. This new weapon will not have any connection to radiation. Israel is developing many sophisticated weapons and must share this knowledge with the USA because Israel doesn't have the finances or the capability to develop or manufacture them. These new weapons will be easy to move because they will be more compact, and I heard these words in the night vision: Miniaturize and Compartmentalize.

Soon, nuclear weapons and armed attack missiles will become obsolete. Electronics will play a major role in warfare, along with new weapons of technology. Israel will soon lead the world in science, disease cures and much advancement.

Angel With Gifts

March 11, 2013

After the word about God's wealth, I went back to bed to ponder and sleep. I saw a vision of an angel walking the earth with something in his hand, and I said, "What is that?" I then looked again and saw that it was a huge horn of plenty, and he was walking the earth, giving all manner of gifts to His remnant people. Many blessings he would give and sometimes He would just pour them out. After the angel left me, there were gifts he had placed in my hands and huge boxes were gift wrapped at my feet. Then I began to feel warm all over—almost hot.

Note: This is connected under prophecy "Christians and Jews" to "My Wealth" 03-13-13

Pockets of Devastation

October 22, 2013

I was on my way back to Philadelphia on the train from Washington, D.C. In a restful state -not quite asleep- I had a vision. It was as though there were pockets of devastation across the U.S. Nobody lived in those areas; it was totally devastated. I got the word, "calamity"…not knowing whether it was a natural calamity or if it was from an uprising against the Government. Possibly, a pocket of war where people had risen up outside the U.S. and we fought them. But it was total destruction. It was not safe to go there.

Then what I saw of the rest of U.S. was fine—people appeared normal and moving about their business feeling secure. But I noticed that people in the U.S. were not flying very much like they had in the past. They were travelling mostly by car, bus or train.

It made me stop and think of the prophecy we had of things going back to the way they were in the 40s, 50s, and 60s. People were often travelling by car, bus or train, even though airplanes were available. So I see it going back to that. It also made me think of the dream I had when I came to my hometown in Tennessee. I was transported into the town and I saw that the courthouse and the downtown had been burned down. I saw a young man there, about 30 years old. I was looking up the street toward my house and told him that I always went there when visiting. I told him I was going to go take a look, and he told me that everything was destroyed. Everything had been devastated. Everything's devastated, he kept repeating. He said to do what I wanted but mentioned that it got worse farther up. So I didn't go.

October 23, 2013

I had another vision… It was much the same as the one described above; however, the pockets of devastation and destruction were much closer together. It seemed like the destruction was three times worse. And I knew that the vision was of China.

October 24, 2013

I awoke out of a dream where I saw pockets of devastation all over Mexico. The devastation was much worse than in China and the U.S.

The Lord spoke the word, "calamity" and, I feel this devastation in the U.S., China and Mexico was brought on by a natural calamity such as an earthquake.

Ash Fallout

June 25 2014

Last night, I had a dream that we were at home watching television and were being warned to not go outside for three to five days until it was safe. Only emergency people with the proper masks and equipment should go outside. We looked out the window to see huge snow-like flakes that were a grayish-white color covering everything in about two to three inches. It was strange to see. All we could discern was that it was ash from a volcano like the still active ones in Yellowstone National Park.

June 26, 2014

I dreamed I was storing food, toilet paper, and general household supplies/clothes. I had been told to store enough for five years.

Also, I had more dreams all night long that the things the Lord had been showing us were going to begin. From July forward, it will be a very dangerous time on the earth from natural disaster to war. (No, it's not climate change or global warming, which is a hoax, a fraud. See Prophecy, "Chicken Little.")

Lastly, for weeks I have been having the impression of a huge earthquake from Memphis, Tennessee up and down the Mississippi River. The New Madrid Fault Line. There were several earthquakes in December 1811 and January 1812 that formed a 20,000-acre lake, Reelfoot Lake, in northwest Tennessee, close to the Mississippi River.

New Birth

Today if you realize that you really don't know God the Father and His Son Jesus Christ who died on the cross for your sins it is time to take the first step of faith. He would like to be your Lord and Savior today. To experience the New Birth also called being Born Again you must repent, confess you are a sinner and decide to turn from your old life and gods and dedicate your whole being to Jesus Christ. You are then promised a new life in heaven not hell. You must confess Jesus Christ before man. The Holy Bible is very clear when it says there is <u>only one way</u> to God the Father and that is by the shed blood of Jesus Christ. We are a human spirit which is dead to God and must be reborn. Read these scriptures in the Holy Bible and then pray to receive Jesus as your Lord and Savior. John 3:7, John 3:16, Romans 8:14-16, John 3:36, Acts 3:19 2 Corinthians 3:17, Ephesians 2:8-9 and 1 Peter 1:23..

To grow in your relationship with God you need to find a good church family. We recommend visiting a few local churches before deciding on a church home. If you're not sure where to start, visit www.arcchurches.com/find-a-church or www.kcm.org/church-listing to locate a church near you.

While you are looking for a church home, you can watch great messages to build your faith today! Simple visit. www.strongfaithchurch.org.

If you asked Jesus into your heart, need prayer, have a comment or would like to make cash or check donations please write to him at the address below.

Robert T. Claiborne is available to speak at your next meeting, conference, TV or radio program.

Robert is affiliated with The Missionary Church International Columbia, South Carolina, USA

Robert T. Claiborne Ministries
E-mail: roberttclaiborneministries@gmail.com
P.O. Box 63
Wayne, Penn. 19087- 0063
U.S.A.

God Is Speaking

As a mother, you have the opportunity to mold minds, nurture growth and develop potential, like no one else. You are a mother! Jochebed raised three leaders. She was a housewife, living in slavery, yet she trained and led her children into the purpose of God for their lives.

How did Leah Cope? A substitute bride! She used the hurt and heartache of life as preparation for her future, not allowing the pain to consume her and make her bitter.

The greatest playwright of the day has not equaled the drama of her life. Growing up under the shadow of her beautiful sister, betrayed by her father, rejected and unloved by her husband. Surely, we can all relate to something in this woman's life!

Books Published by Women of God Ministries

All titles are available in paperback and download editions on Amazon.com
For more information, visit: www.wogministries.com

Victorious Christian Living Today!

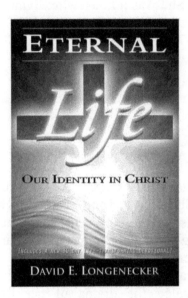

Eternal Life Our Identity in Christ reveals secrets you need to know for victorious Christian living. In order to reach your divine destiny, you must understand your divine identity. Jesus has provided much more in redemption than most Christians are aware. When you know what eternal life is and provides, the miraculous becomes a common occurrence in your life. In *Eternal Life Our Identity in Christ*, you will discover how to:

- Change your destiny by discovering your true identity.
- Understand your spiritual authority like never before.
- Live above sin, sickness, and Satan.
- Step out daily in the dominion of God.
- Develop an incredible sense of dignity and worth.

Discover how you were meant to live. The truths within this book will transform your every experience with God. Guaranteed!

For more information visit
www.delministries.org

NOTES: